British
Language & Culture

British Language & Culture
2nd edition – March 2007
First published – June 1999

Published by
Lonely Planet Publications Pty Ltd ABN 36 005 607 983
90 Maribyrnong St, Footscray, Victoria 3011, Australia

Lonely Planet Offices
Australia Locked Bag 1, Footscray, Victoria 3011
USA 150 Linden St, Oakland CA 94607
UK 72-82 Rosebery Ave, London, EC1R 4RW

Cover
British montage by Yukiyoshi Kamimura
© Lonely Planet Publications Pty Ltd 2007

ISBN 978 1 86450 286 2

text © Lonely Planet Publications Pty Ltd 2007

10 9 8 7 6 5 4 3 2

Printed by C&C Offset Printing Co Ltd, China

ACKNOWLEDGMENTS

Editor Vanessa Battersby would like to acknowledge the following people for their contributions to this phrasebook:

David Else for restructuring, updating and rewriting this new edition of the book. David is the author of Lonely Planet's guidebooks to Britain and England, and many other titles. A Londoner by origin, David migrated north via Wiltshire, Bristol, Cardiff and Derbyshire and now lives in Yorkshire. David has a degree in English Literature, an interest in linguistics, and a passion for regional dialects or odd colloquialisms wherever they are found. David would like to give heartfelt thanks first to his wife, Corinne, who read through the manuscript and made numerous suggestions. Many thanks also go to his multi-dialectical friends and colleagues, spread across England, Wales, Scotland, America, Australia and elsewhere, who between them advised him on topics ranging from sport, food and music, to history, slang and swearwords: Heather Dickson, Tom Parkinson, Jacqui Cook, Roy Thompson, Tom Hall, Ray Bartlett, Neil Wilson, Becky Ohlsen and Fayette Fox. In-house at LP Melbourne, thanks go to the editorial team of Ben Handicott, Karin Vidstrup Monk and Vanessa Battersby.

Thanks also to Vicki Webb, editor, and authors Dr Elizabeth Bartsch-Parker, Stephen Burgen and Dominic Watt, along with contributors Dr Roibeard O Maolalaigh (on Scottish Gaelic) and Richard Crowe (on Welsh), for their work on the first edition this book was based upon.

Lonely Planet Language Products

Publishing Manager: Chris Rennie

Commissioning Editors: Karin Vidstrup Monk & Ben Handicott

Editor: Vanessa Battersby

Assisting Editor: Francesca Coles

Layout Designer: Pablo Gastar & Indra Kilfoyle

Cartographer: Wayne Murphy

Project Manager: Adam McCrow

Managing Editor: Annelies Mertens

Acting Layout Manager: Kate McDonald

Series Designer: Yukiyoshi Kamimura

Contents

Regional variations 159

Regional languages 203

Wordfinder 235

Index 253

Maps

CONTENTS

5

Great Britain

SHORT HISTORY

English is one of the most widely spoken languages on earth, and the closest thing we have to a global common tongue. It's the international language of science, business, aviation, technology and the internet – not to mention much of the international sporting circuit. It's the language of global cinema, and if you want to make it big in popular music, you generally sing in English – wherever you come from.

As recently as the end of the 18th century, however, the majority of English speakers still lived in England. Originally derived from the dialects of obscure northern European tribes, English became the language of Britain around the middle of the first millennium AD.

Today, English is the first language of around 400 million people globally, and the second language of perhaps 400 million more. It's the national language, official language or common language in more than 60 countries. In many parts of the world English is the preferred second language – it's the second language of choice of European school students, for example, by a large margin.

As English was exported across the world, this once minor language developed into many different forms, so that the English spoken in America is different to that spoken in Australia, the English spoken in Ireland is different to that spoken in India, and so on – and they're all different to the mother tongue that spawned them.

This book is about British English – the English spoken by around 57 million people on the island of Britain. This may be the birthplace of English, but the language here certainly isn't static. The British take great pleasure in using the English language fully and inventively, and it continues to evolve and be exploited – sometimes with amusing results. For example, British politicians don't lie, they *dissemble*; kids aren't simply surprised, they're *gobsmacked*; football fans suffering a defeat aren't just sad, they're *as sick as a parrot*.

On it goes – British English is a tirelessly inventive language, borrowing without shame, outrageously playful, always seeking simplicity and yet revelling in complexity. We hope this book helps you enjoy the language as much as we do.

WHAT'S IN A NAME?

This book is about British English. The state of *Great Britain* is made up of three separate countries – England, Wales and Scotland. England is the dominant country, but the peoples of Scotland and Wales have kept a strong sense of national identity (perhaps precisely because of English dominance).

It's important to remember that the terms *Great Britain* and *England* refer to different political entities; they're not interchangeable, and to say *England* when you mean *Britain* could cause offence if you're in Wales or Scotland. Scotland has a separate parliament and church, plus its own systems of law, banking and education; Wales has its own National Assembly – although it doesn't enjoy as much autonomy as the Scottish parliament.

Just for the record, the *United Kingdom* (*UK*) consists of Great Britain, Northern Ireland and some semiautonomous islands such as the Isle of Man. The island of Ireland consists of Northern Ireland and the Republic of Ireland (also called *Eire*). And for you scholars out there, *the British Isles* is a *geographical* term for the whole group of islands that make up the UK and the Republic of Ireland. The more politically correct term is *Britain and Ireland*.

Beginnings

Britain may be a small island on the edge of Europe, but its history has been far from insular. Over the millennia, waves of invaders and incomers arrived, settled and made their mark – and were (eventually) absorbed.

The same thing happened to the English language. In the 15 centuries of its existence, English has been notable for its openness to other languages, and its readiness to adopt, absorb or adapt foreign words. Take, for example, the various ways of describing the coming together of two or more people. It could be a *rendezvous* or a *reunion* (both borrowed from French); a *gathering* or *meeting* (both originally Old English); an *assignation* or *encounter* or *rally* or *tryst* (Old French); a *caucus* (Native American Algonquin) or a *powwow* (Native American Narragansett). Together, they allow the speaker a remarkable degree of precision about the kind of 'meeting'.

For another example, just look at the nautical lexicon. Dutch has contributed *cruise*, *deck*, *freebooter* and *yacht*. The words *armada* and *galleon* are borrowed from Spanish, *buccaneer* and *frigate* come from French, *capsize* comes from Catalan, *kayak* from Inuit languages and *catamaran* from Tamil.

Before we go on to look at this fondness for borrowing in more detail, however, let's go back to the very beginnings of English.

NEW ARRIVALS

The withdrawal of the last Roman troops from Britain in 410 AD heralded another invasion, this one by the Angles and Saxons – Teutonic tribes from northern Europe, often lumped together by historians as Anglo-Saxons. They moved fast, and quickly absorbed or drove out most of the Romano-British inhabitants, introducing their own culture and language so thoroughly that by the late 6th century the country now called England was predominantly Anglo-Saxon.

The language of the Anglo-Saxons was the earliest form of English, and is now known as Old English. Linguists estimate that out of English's vast vocabulary only around 4300 words are derived from Old English, but these words are so basic – for example *at*, *child*, *drink*, *for*, *go*, *God*, *live*, *love*, *man*, *to* and *woman* – that they make up the bulk of everyday speech.

In fact, nearly all of the 100 most commonly used words in modern English are of Anglo-Saxon origin. Take something fundamental like a *door*. Not only the term *door*, but also most of the associated words are Old or Middle English – *ajar*, *close*, *frame*, *handle*, *hinge*, *key*, *knob*, *lock*, *open*, *panel* and *sill*. Only a few terms are borrowed from other languages – *jamb* (from French) and *architrave* (Italian), for example.

MISSIONARY MEN

The Angles and Saxons were pagans, and their invasion forced the Christian religion of the Romano-British people to the edges of the British Isles – to Wales, Scotland and Ireland. The Pope of the time, Gregory I, decided this was a poor show, and in AD 597 sent missionaries to Britain. This also had the effect of introducing words of Latin (the language of the Christian Church) into English. *Angel*, *candle* and *disciple* were all adopted during this period.

A CUTE ANGLE

Of the missionaries sent to Britain in the 6th century, one holy pioneer was St Augustine, who successfully converted Angles in the area now covered by the modern county of Kent. Some good-looking specimens were sent to Rome as proof of Augustine's progress – giving rise to Pope Gregory's famous quip *Non Angli sed angeli* ('not Angles, more like angels').

THE VIKINGS

The missionaries weren't the only early arrivals to the new Anglo-Saxon Britain. By around the 7th century, the *Vikings* – a catch-all term for the Norse or Nordic peoples from Scandinavia – had started to loom on the horizon.

School history books give the impression that Vikings turned up, killed everyone, took everything and left. While there's some truth in that, many Vikings settled in Britain for good.

There were two main waves of Viking invaders. The first came from the area now called Norway, and they attacked northern Scotland and the parts of northern England that are now Cumbria and Lancashire. By around AD 850 a second wave, from Denmark, had conquered and occupied east and northeast England, making the city of Yorvik (now called York) their capital.

From their northern territories, the Vikings then spread across central England until they were confronted by Anglo-Saxon armies coming from the south, led by the new king of Wessex, Alfred the Great. The battles which followed were seminal in the foundation of the nation-state of England, and although they didn't all go Alfred's way, by 886 he had managed to push the Vikings back to the north.

Their linguistic legacy is still evident in parts of Scotland and northern England in the place names and local dialects. Examples include places ending in:

- *-by* (from the Norse for 'farm', 'homestead' or 'settlement') such as *Grimsby* or *Derby*
- *-thorp* (another word for 'settlement' or 'village') as in *Althorp* or *Scunthorpe*
- *-thwaite* (a cleared piece of land) as in *Braithwaite* or *Longthwaite*
- *-toft* (an area of land) as in *Lowestoft*

Family names ending in *-son* (meaning, of course, 'son of') are also a Viking legacy.

In addition to names, the Vikings brought many everyday terms such as *dregs*, *egg*, *husband*, *knife*, *law*, *root*, *sly*, *take* and *window*. English also adopted the Norse pronouns *they*, *them* and *their*. Old English already had the word *home* (with the same meaning it has today), but took on the Nordic word *house* as well – an early indicator of the preference for two or more words with the same broad meaning when the new word allows a different nuance to be expressed.

In total, around 1000 words of modern English have Nordic origins, and the further north you go in Britain and Ireland, the more words of Norse origin survive. In the Shetland Islands, north of Scotland, as many as 1500 words of Old Norse remain in use.

FRIDAY ON MY MIND

Interestingly, the Vikings had the same gods as the Anglo-Saxons, so the days of the week were unaffected by the invasions. They were named after the sun and moon (*Sunday* and *Monday*), the Anglo-Saxon gods Tiw, Woden, Thunor and Frige (*Tuesday*, *Wednesday*, *Thursday*, *Friday*), and the Roman god Saturn (*Saturday*). The names of the months in English, by contrast, generally have Latin roots.

Beginnings

THE NORMANS

Life remained unsettled for a few more centuries in England, as the royal pendulum swung between Anglo-Saxon and Danish-Viking monarchs. When King Edward the Confessor died, the crown passed to Harold, his brother-in-law. That should've settled things, but Edward had a cousin in Normandy (in today's France) called William, who thought *he* should have succeeded to the throne of England.

The end result was the Battle of Hastings in 1066, the most memorable of dates for anyone who's studied British history – and for many who haven't. William sailed from France with an army of Norman soldiers, the Saxons were defeated, and Harold was killed – according to tradition by an arrow in the eye. William became king of England, earning himself the prestigious title 'William the Conqueror'.

The arrival of William the Conqueror was a milestone event, as it marked the end of Britain's linguistic and cultural ties to the Nordic countries (only in Orkney and Shetland did the Viking presence continue until the 15th century). Mainland Britain's focus shifted to France, western Europe and the Mediterranean, with massive linguistic and cultural implications. In addition, the Norman landing capped an era of armed invasion. Britain has not been seriously invaded by a foreign power in the 900-odd years since 1066.

CLASS OF 66

After the Norman conquest of England, a strict hierarchy developed. At the top was the monarch, below that the nobles (barons, bishops, dukes and earls), then knights and lords, and at the bottom were peasants or *serfs*, effectively indentured labourers. This hierarchy, known as the *feudal system*, was the basis of the class system which still exists in Britain today.

STATION TO STATION

The word *Charing* in the name of London's Charing Cross train station derives from a borrowed French term, *Chère Reine*, meaning 'dear queen'. When King Edward I's wife Eleanor died in 1290, the grief-stricken monarch ordered memorial crosses to be placed everywhere her funeral procession rested on its way from Nottinghamshire to London. One of these points was Charing Cross – a reproduction cross stands in the courtyard of the station today.

In the years after the Norman invasion, the French-speaking Norman rulers and most of their English-speaking Saxon subjects kept to themselves. As with the Vikings, the invasion didn't eradicate the English language, although it had a huge effect on it. For around three centuries French was the official language, and English was virtually ignored by the educated elite of the church and state. As a result, as many as 10,000 modern English words are derived from Norman French. Most linguists believe that it was probably during this period, when English was left in the hands of the common people, that the process of simplifying it and stripping down its grammar began to accelerate.

Obvious examples of French borrowings are the terms of law and government, such as *adultery*, *court*, *justice*, *marriage*, *parliament*, *sovereign* and *tyrant*.

In later centuries, perhaps thanks to the *feudal system* (see the box on page 12), English helped itself to the rich store of French words devised to express class distinctions, among them *arriviste*, *bourgeois*, *chauffeur*, *chauvinism*, *elite*, *faux pas*, *limousine*, *nouveau riche* and *parvenu*. The word *snobbery* itself is English, of course.

Even in modern times, no one has ever accused the English of being *chic*, and they've had to ransack French *bon mots* in order to acquire some *élan* and *panache*, or affect a *blasé veneer* of *je ne sais quoi* to cover their confusion over what is in *vogue* and what is *passé*.

Beginnings

13

Recent history

Despite the fact that Britain has not been successfully invaded since 1066, the English language has kept on borrowing from anywhere and everywhere. Centuries of sea-borne trade, crusades and, later, the British Empire, ensured that the British travelled around the world, both exporting their language and importing foreign words into it as they went. Without borrowing, the British wouldn't now be sitting in their *pyjamas* (Urdu), living in *bungalows* (Hindi) or smoking *hashish* (Arabic) – and there would be another name for *assassins* (Arabic via the French *hachichien*).

There are thousands more words, borrowed over the centuries and now firmly part of mainstream English, like:

anorak	(Inuit)
intelligentsia	(Russian)
sauna	(Finnish)
taboo	(Tongan)
thug	(Hindi)
tycoon	(Japanese)

English doesn't borrow only from faraway languages, of course. Words in English derived from Scottish Gaelic, for example, include:

English	Gaelic	Meaning
bard	bard	poet
bog	bog	soft, wet
brogue	bròg	shoe
caber	cabar	pole
claymore	claidheamh mòr	big sword
dune	dùn	heap
galore	gu leòr	plenty

British English is still borrowing from other languages. In the global village, new words rush into English within a matter of weeks, especially whenever there's some upheaval in a foreign land. First they refer only to events in the place they came from – *glasnost* and *perestroika*, for example, initially referred only to political changes in the former Soviet Union during the 1990s – but soon they enter the language in their own right. At one time you might have heard a British government official say something like 'It's time there was a little more glasnost in the Ministry of Trade.' Not all borrowed words enter the vocabulary permanently, though – time moves on, and these Russian words no longer form part of everyday speech.

More recently, a number of Arabic or Islamic terms – such as *fatwa*, *intifada* and *jihad* – have been adopted and adapted for domestic consumption.

Alongside the constant shifts in vocabulary, the English accent keeps on developing too. The clipped vowels and consonants of 1930s newsreels are a thing of the past of course, but even the voices on TV and radio 20 years ago sound dated today.

A notable development in the 1960s was the rise of *Estuary English*, a hybrid dialect between the original Cockney of London and standard English. It's called 'Estuary' because it developed with the new towns along the banks of the Thames Estuary to the east of London, as part of the capital's post-war expansion. Today, Estuary English is very widely spoken across much of south and southeast England. (For more details see page 165.)

An even more recent trend of spoken British English is the tendency to end statements with an upward inflection, making them sound like questions. This rising intonation is thought to have been introduced from Australian and New Zealand English, where it's common, via popular Australian soap operas such as *Neighbours* and *Home and Away*.

Features of English

The key features of the English language include borrowing, layering, flexibility and simplification. This section looks at some of these aspects in more detail, as they help explain many of the modern developments in British English.

BORROWING

Borrowing is a major feature of the English language – in fact, it is generally believed that English contains more loanwords than any other language.

Borrowing generally occurs when existing words are inadequate or too restricting. For example, as we mentioned earlier, English is happy with Anglo-Saxon terms for the basics of building (*brick*, *door*, *roof*, *wall*, *window*), but for the finer points of architecture it has turned to Italian – *capital*, *corridor*, *cupola*, *dome*, *mezzanine*, *portico* etc.

Once foreign words are imported, of course, English takes what seems to be a random approach to their pronunciation. Many foreign words keep their original pronunciation, or something like it. For example, British English speakers follow the French pronunciation for *parquet* and *rendezvous* (pronounced 'parkay' and 'rondayvoo'). But for the word *repartee* the Brits ignore the French and pronounce it as 'repartee', not 'repartay'. (Incidentally, in American English *repartee* is pronounced 'repartay'. See the Misunderstandings chapter for more on British and American differences.)

Similarly, British English has borrowed the word *marijuana* from Spanish without altering the spelling or pronunciation very much, but the word *guerrilla* is nearly always pronounced 'gerila' (not 'gereelya' as in Spanish) – which doesn't help distinguish freedom fighters from large primates. Other Spanish words, however, have been totally anglicised – *cucaracha* and *cocodrilo*, for example, have become *cockroach* and *crocodile*. Sometimes the Brits can't even decide which pronunciation to favour. For example, the first letter of the word *junta* can be pronounced both *j* (as in 'junk') and *h* (as in 'hunt' – from the Spanish pronunciation).

LAYERING

English has been termed a 'layered language' – meaning there's often a choice between a simple native English word and another one of foreign origin (usually from French, Latin or Greek), which usually expresses a different nuance of meaning. For example, you can choose to *make* something (from Old English), but if that's too general a word, there's always the option of using *manufacture* (Latin via Italian) or *synthesise* (Greek) instead. You can *speak* or *say* something (Old English) or, if you want to be taken more seriously, you can *communicate* or *converse* (Latin). Latin and Greek were the languages of education for centuries and still have erudite overtones. Even today, whenever people feel that what they have to say is important – such as when giving evidence in court or appearing on TV – they burst out with words and constructions of Latin and Greek origin, usually at the expense of clarity.

There are also many instances where an English noun has a Latin adjective – as in *earth* and *terrestrial*, *horse* and *equestrian*.

FLEXIBILITY

The flexibility and sheer size of the English lexicon, with numerous words for the same thing and numerous words sounding the same, means wordplay has been a major feature of the language for centuries. Fourteenth-century writer Chaucer certainly took advantage, as did Shakespeare – he alone is credited with creating hundreds of idioms (such as *cold comfort*, *cruel to be kind*, *foul play*, *mind's eye*, *one fell swoop*, *poisoned chalice*) which have remained in everyday use for 400 years.

Many other expressions entered the language from the Authorised or King James Version of the Bible, translated in the 17th century, and are still with us today, including *salt of the earth*, *skin of your teeth*, *sour grapes* and *suffer fools gladly*.

As well as wordplay and idioms, English can produce new terms simply by combining old ones or placing them side by side. In the current era, for example, an entire shorthand vocabulary has been developed by tabloid newspapers. It's doubtful that other languages could produce bizarre British tabloid terms such as *drug fiend*, *gymslip mum*, *love rat*, *porn king*, *sex romp* or *tug-of-love child*.

SIMPLIFICATION

While on the one hand English has ceaselessly expanded its vocabulary, on the other hand it has simplified its grammar, stripping down the engine of language to basic components wherever possible.

Old English was (as many modern languages still are) an 'inflected' language, meaning words changed form not only according to things like tense but according to their function, the relationship between the person speaking and the person addressed and so on. Old English had – like modern German – three genders. Nouns had numerous 'cases' (different forms depending on their function in a sentence), and there were as many as 11 forms of adjectives. By the end of the 14th century, however, English had simply dumped most of the complex inflections, cases and genders.

Instead of having the word-ending change to clarify how a word related to others in a sentence, English employed a range of simple prepositions – *at*, *from*, *in*, *to*, *with* and so on.

Gender was simply dropped. English accepts that it's useful to distinguish between a man and a woman, or a cow and a bull, but decided there was no reason to allocate a gender to objects and activities with no sexual characteristics. Does it add anything to a language to give a crankshaft or an omelette a gender? Not really. So English uses just 'a' and 'the', not pairs like *un* and *une* and *le* and *la* as in French, and most nouns (apart from things like bulls and cows) are refreshingly neutral.

In the same way, English has sometimes dispensed with words that make no useful distinction, and when there's little danger of the listener getting the wrong message. For example, French feels it necessary to distinguish between 'to know' in the sense of acquaintance (*connaître*) – 'I know Charlie very well' – and 'to know' in the sense of knowledge (*savoir*) – 'I know how to play the piano.' English is content with the one verb.

GETTING ON

In its drive towards simplification, probably the greatest achievement of the English language was the invention of the phrasal verb – the combination of a verb and a preposition or adverb to achieve a new meaning.

The word *get* is the best example. It's an Old English survivor with a basic meaning of 'obtain', but this is only its part-time job. It spends the rest of its life joined to other words creating phrasal verbs and a host of new meanings:

You *get up* and *get out of* bed, and remember you *got out of* your head last night again – which is *getting to be* a drag because it makes it so hard *to get started* in the mornings. You can hardly *get on* your *get-up* and *get out of* the house. You *get* the bus to work and your boss, who you *don't get along with*, *gets on your case*: he just *doesn't get* that *you've got a life* (and hasn't from the *get go*). He *gets over* it though and you *get on with* things and the day *gets* better – well, you *get by* at least, even if all you think about is *getting out of* there.

Phrasal verbs today form the basis of everyday speech and are the key to the structural simplicity of the language. They're also the bane of foreign students learning English, firstly because there are so many of them and secondly because they have to be learned by heart. There's no way you could deduce that you *get on* and *get off* a train, boat or plane, but *get in* and *get out of* a car.

FEELING SHEEPISH

One of the few relics of the Old English system of inflection is plurals such as *children*, *men*, *women* and *feet*. And then there are the odd ones – *deer*, *fish*, *sheep* – that don't have a separate plural form at all, and seem to be there for no other reason than to make foreigners look stupid when they say 'sheeps'.

Likewise French is loath to mix up the temporary and immutable facts of existence. So you say 'I am (*être*) a woman' but 'I have (*avoir*) hunger.' English considers such distinctions unnecessary and assumes that people saying 'I'm thirsty' will not be misunderstood as meaning they are always (and will forever be) thirsty. However, just to keep everyone on their toes, English *does* feel a need to distinguish between other things, like *hearing* and *listening*, or *looking* and *seeing*.

Another clever trick is to employ an army of simple prefixes and suffixes (eg *dis-*, *pre-*, *re-*, *-y*) to alter the sense of a word. Negation can be expressed through the application of *a-*, *anti-*, *ir-*, *non-*, *in-*, *il-*, *un* and so on. Adjectives can be converted to nouns using *-ness*, nouns into adjectives using *-ible*, and adverbs created using *-ably*.

Standard English has also done away with informal and formal forms of address. In German, for example, there are seven forms of the word 'you'. In English, you don't have to worry about where you stand in relation to someone else or what degree of respect they should be shown – everyone is simply *you*. English is very economical in its use of definite or indefinite articles, too: you can say 'I'm going to bed' or 'I don't want lunch' or 'It's Derby day', where other languages would require articles (*the* bed, *the* lunch, *the* day of *the* Derby).

VERSATILITY

Another aspect of English is its tendency to let the same word do service as a noun or a verb (eg *drink*, *love*, *push*, *smoke*). Its versatility also allows English to make one word from two (*coathanger*, *doorknob*, *handbook*) – although only to form simple compounds. Long or unwieldy compounds such as those favoured by German (like *Gewerkschaftsbewegung*, meaning 'trade union movement') generally don't appear. English prefers to keep the words separate.

One problem with versatility, however, is inconsistency. Take the adjectival form of nouns. Here's what looks like a nice simple pattern:

clamour	**clamorous**
glamour	**glamorous**
humour	**humorous**

But look what happens elsewhere:

colour	**colourful**
favour	**favourite**
savour	**savoury**
splendour	**splendid**

Despite wonderful simplifications in some areas, English sometimes seems to play about with words for no particular reason.

WHEN MORE IS MORE

To the question, 'How many words do you need?', English replies, 'How many have you got?' It never seems to have enough. Calculations vary according to how 'an English word' is defined, but range from about 100,000 to over a million. The *Oxford English Dictionary* contains around 600,000 words.

Around 1950, linguists produced Basic English, a stripped-down version of the language with a vocabulary of just 850 words. There's nothing you can't say in Basic English, but that hasn't stopped anyone using the other 599,150.

METAPHORICALLY SPEAKING

The English language has a special love affair with metaphor. Every industry, every sport, every form of endeavour generates its own vocabulary, and as soon as this happens it's mined for metaphors.

Take, for example, the military and naval spheres. Before you even start to *drum up* support for your *campaign*, you must *nail your colours to the mast*. Then you need to *set your sights* on a *united front*, *steering clear* of *loose cannons* or *camp followers* and anyone likely to *break ranks* under their *baptism of fire*. You need to *recruit* only those who'll *stick to their guns*, even if they *get caught in the crossfire* in *no-man's land*.

And that's only a start. Even if you've never been involved in the sports of boxing or wrestling (and very few people have), you may still have *stepped into the ring* or found yourself *on the ropes*, talking *a good fight* but unable to *box clever* and forced to *slug it out* with some *heavyweight* who doesn't *pull their punches*. You have to learn to take the *body blows* and *roll with the punches* and hope to be *saved by the bell*, because if you can't *punch above your weight* you'll be *out for the count*. It's either that or *take a dive* or *throw in the towel*.

In the same way, hunting has given us *cut to the chase*, *open season*, *sitting duck* and *stalking horse*. From the animal kingdom comes *a game of cat and mouse*, *penguin suit*, *snake in the grass*, *stubborn as a mule*, *water off a duck's back* and so on. Even plant-life has supplied *lily-livered*, *pansy*, *shrinking violet* and *wallflower*. The English appetite for metaphor appears insatiable.

SPEAKING BRITISH ENGLISH

This chapter will guide you through some of the quirks of British English grammar and pronunciation, then delve deeper into the peculiarities of etiquette, body language and conversations about that most British of topics – the weather.

Pronunciation

As seen in the Short History chapter, a major feature of the English language is its propensity to borrow words from other languages around the world. The English language has also travelled abroad over the centuries – to Australasia, the Americas, India, parts of Africa, the Caribbean and many more places – and developed separately in each area.

The result: the same words are often pronounced differently in Britain and in other English-speaking countries. The difference may lie in which syllable of a word is emphasised, how a vowel is pronounced, or even which consonant is used.

The selection of everyday English words given below have the same spelling and the same meaning in Britain, Australia, America and other English-speaking countries, but are pronounced differently. (See the Misunderstandings chapter for words that have different *meanings* in different countries.)

borough	the British English pronunciation is 'burah', not 'buroh'
clerk	pronounced 'clark'
decade	*de*cade (not 'de*cade*')
era	'eera', the first syllable rhymes with 'ear' (it is not pronounced 'era', as in the US, with the *e* pronounced as in 'egg')
fillet	'fillet' (the *t* is pronounced)
glacial	'glayshul' – the first *a* is pronounced to rhyme with 'hay'

WHICH ROUTE?

The word *route*, as in 'the route from London to Brighton', is pronounced 'root' in British English. In American English, it's spelt 'route' but usually pronounced to rhyme with 'pout' (although in some parts of New England the British pronunciation is still favoured). The word 'rout' – ie, a crushing defeat – is pronounced to rhyme with 'pout' in both British and American English. To add to the confusion, the first syllable of *router*, a woodworking implement, also rhymes with 'pout' in both British and American English. Then there's the *router*, a computer peripheral. Some British techies pronounce it 'rooter', to distinguish it from the carpenter's tool, while others favour the rhyme-with-'pout' option, influenced perhaps by American colleagues. The American pronunciation seems to be quite a new development; as recently as the 1960s, when Chuck Berry first sang about iconic US highway Route 66, he definitely rhymed it with 'root'.

glacier	'glasier' – the *a* pronounced as in 'crass'
herb	the *h* is pronounced in British English
hostel	'*host*ul' – the second syllable is *not* the same as in 'hotel'
hostile	'hostyle' – the second syllable rhymes with 'style' (also in *sterile* and *fertile*)
medicine	often 'medsin' – notice, only two syllables
nauseous	'nawseus' – three syllables, not two as in American English
pasta	'pasta' – the first syllable rhymes with 'mass'
penchant	pronounced like the French, 'ponshon'
privacy	'privasee' – the *i* pronounced as in 'bit'
private	'praivat' – *i* as in 'eye'
schedule	'shedyual' – not 'skedyual' as in American English
sexual	'seksyual' or 'sekshual'
urinal	'yurainal' – the *i* pronounced as in 'wine'

vaginal	'vajainal' – the *i* as in 'wine'
vitamin	'vitamin' – *i* pronounced as in 'fit'
yogurt	'yogurt' – *o* pronounced as in 'hot'
z	the letter *z* is pronounced 'zed', not 'zee' as in the US
zebra	'zebra' to rhyme with 'Debra'

Grammar

The grammar of standard British English doesn't differ much from the grammar of other varieties of the English language, such as US English and Australian English, and there's very little that's likely to cause misunderstandings. Dialects of British English which do use different grammar rules are discussed in the Regional Variations chapter.

SORTED FOR E'S

In English, not only are the same letters often pronounced differently, but the same sounds can be written several different ways. There are at least 11, yes 11, different ways of writing the sound 'ee' in English, including:

donk**ey**	L**ei**gh	mumm**y**	p**ae**diatrician
p**ee**p	p**eo**ple	p**ie**ce	r**ea**d
rec**ei**ve	r**ei**terate	spec**i**ality	

Part of the problem is that English has a habit of borrowing words from other languages and retaining their spelling, but attempts to rationalise English spelling have been passionately resisted. Even now, people in Britain rail against the eminently sensible American practice of dropping the *u* from words such as 'colour' and 'glamour'. Indeed, there's nothing like an innocent Americanism to make most Brits turn purple.

SPELLBOUND

One of the most noticeable differences between the varieties of English is the divide between British English spelling and American English spelling. For example, in Britain, the preferred spelling is *-tre* (not *-ter*):

> *centre*
> *litre*
> *metre*
> *theatre*

Likewise, many words end in *-our*, not *-or*, in British:

> *colour*
> *endeavour*
> *honour*
> *labour*
> *neighbour*
> *savour*

And words which end in *-ize* in the US are generally spelt *-ise* in British English; for example:

> *aggrandise*
> *finalise*
> *pluralise*
> *terrorise*

(In some British publications there's a trend towards using *-ize* – it's not unknown to see 'apologize' or 'capitalize' – but generally American spellings are firmly resisted.)

Other words in British English which are spelt differently in other versions of English (especially in American English) include:

>

aluminium the US version is spelt 'aluminum', with four syllables and the stress on the second ('aloominum'). The British use five syllables ('aloomineeum') or four ('aloominyum') with the stress on the third.

defence spelt 'defense' in the US (although ***defensive*** has an 's' in British English)

draught this word is pronounced 'draft' and relates to the verb 'to draw' meaning 'to pull' – as in a ***draught horse*** (a horse that pulls things) and ***draught beer*** (pulled from the barrel by a pump). It can also mean ***draught*** as in a light air current in a room ('It's draughty in here'). The British use the spelling ***draft*** to mean: 'to conscript' (***to draft someone into the army***); a document used to withdraw money at a bank; and a version of an essay or report (eg a ***first draft***).

furore this is the British equivalent of the American word 'furor'. It's pronounced 'fyuroree' in three syllables.

gaol meaning 'jail' and pronounced that way

kerb British English spelling for 'curb' when it relates to a raised edge on a road. ***Curb*** means 'cut back' in British English.

programme pronounced the same as 'program' is in America

speciality notice the extra *i* making it five syllables – 'spe-shee-a-li-ty'

tonne a metric tonne – 1000kg. The imperial ton (2240lb or 1016kg) is also used in Britain – and not everyone knows the difference. (Both ***ton*** and ***tonne*** are pronounced 'tun' in British English.) Neither should be confused with the US 'short ton' (2000lb).

Grammar

27

Phrasing

British English has some differences in phrasing to other English-speaking countries, where one word – usually a preposition – is different. Below are a few examples.

about   some British English speakers may say 'I looked about me' as an alternative to 'I looked around me'

after   in British English, to ***ask after someone*** is to ask about someone ('I met Jill today, she asked after you')

down to   this means 'the responsibility of' (eg 'It's a good plan, but it's down to the teachers to make it work'). It's not the same as ***up to you*** – see below.

on heat   of an animal, to be in season or in heat ('The cat's on heat')

up to   a phrase that implies a choice ('Stay there, or come with us, it's up to you')

PREPOSITIONAL ANGST

British people dislike American English's propensity to drop the occasional preposition. 'I will write you' makes them wince. Brits prefer 'I will write to you', even though they're perfectly happy with 'I will phone you'. Another difference: Americans say 'he took it in stride' rather than 'he took it in his stride', and 'she won't commit' as an alternative to 'she won't commit herself'. Cue more purple rage on the east side of the Atlantic.

WHAT'S THAT?

Many British people, especially in northern England, use *that* where other English speakers would use 'so' (eg 'The show was that boring, half the audience went to sleep').

Body language

The main feature of British body language is its restraint! When speaking, most Brits are not very effusive or flamboyant, and generally don't touch the people they're speaking to in the way some other cultures might find usual. (A hand on the arm to emphasise a point, for example, or continued gripping of hands after a handshake to emphasise friendship.) Exceptions of course include late nights in the pub when deep embraces and declarations along the lines of *You're my besht mate, you are* seem perfectly normal.

Not only is touching and gesticulating generally avoided, but compared to many other cultures the Brits prefer to have a bit of space around them during a conversation. Standing too close can be misinterpreted as odd or simply forward. And anyone who looks you in the eye too much during a casual chat is definitely *suspect* (ie suspicious).

Handshaking is also restricted in Britain compared to many other cultures. It's usual when two people are being introduced to each other by a third person in a business situation, but is unusual among friends in everyday situations – unlike in France, for example. Outside a business context, the Brits generally don't extend their hand to a stranger with friendly enthusiasm and say, 'Hi, I'm John' as Americans or Aussies might do.

Finally, there's the topic of volume. Brits generally speak more quietly in public (in restaurants, in cafés, on trains and buses) than folks from many other cultures. On the London Underground it's not unusual for complete strangers to raise eyebrows in mutual amusement when booming American voices discussing the Changing of the Guard can be heard from the other end of the carriage. The exception is, of course, when Brits are on their mobile phones; then they're as loud as everyone else.

Greetings

You'll hear numerous colloquial variations on the popular 'hi' around Britain, depending on where you are and who's talking to you.

For instance, in London and the south you'll often hear *Watcha*, while in some northern areas of England you might hear people say *Ay up* as a casual greeting (often pronounced 'ayoop') and *Ta-ra* for 'goodbye' (pronounced 'tarah').

Elsewhere in England you might hear *Ow do?*, an abbreviation of 'How do you do?', or simply *How?* or *Now then*. The 'goodbye' phrase may be something like *Ta-ta* or *Ta-da*. The word *cheers* is also widely used to mean 'goodbye'.

In many areas, including the Midlands, northern England and the southwest, people passing each other on the street say *Are you all right?*, often reduced to *All right?* (this is pronounced differently in different regions: 'all roit' in the southwest; 'oroit' in the Midlands; 'aal reet' further north). The reply to this question is also *All right*, either as a statement (meaning 'Yes, I'm well thank you') or *All right?* as a question (ie 'I'm well thanks, and how are you?').

If you're greeted with a regional expression you're unfamiliar with in Britain, it's usually best to just say 'hello' or -'hi' in return. If you feel obliged to answer the apparent question, just say 'Fine, thanks' (in the same way as you always reply in the affirmative when people say 'How are you?', even if you've got a broken leg or are recovering from measles). Attempts to use the local vernacular may be interpreted as mockery, and in extreme cases you might *end up chewing gravel* (meaning 'reach the end of the encounter with a punch in the mouth' – from the witty challenge *You looking for trouble or chewing gravel? Either way you'll lose your teeth*).

LITTLE MESTERS

The term *master* was historically applied to a man skilled as an artisan or craft-worker – someone who had 'mastered' their trade. In the city of Sheffield in northern England – once famous worldwide for its steel – skilled metal-workers known as *little mesters* (*mester* being the regional pronunciation of 'master') worked in tiny workshops or corners of factories in the industrial areas, hand-crafting cutlery and small tools. In their heyday, there were thousands of little mesters. By the 1960s this had dwindled to about 20. Very few remain today.

Etiquette

EVERYDAY FORMS OF ADDRESS

When speaking to strangers, or in formal situations, the most common terms of address are *Mr* and *Mrs*. The term *Miss* (originally meaning an unmarried woman, now more often used for young women) is also commonly used. The neutral term *Ms* has yet to be widely adopted in Britain.

The British have a reputation for being reserved, and the use of *Mr* or *Mrs* is common with strangers or on first meeting (although this is not to say first names are never used). Still, it's a good rule *not* to use a person's first name unless you've been invited to or that's the way they've been introduced. Even when you're a patron or customer, formal address is more common. If your friendly hotel receptionist wears the name tag 'John Smith', for example, call him 'Mr Smith', not 'John'.

Here are some other terms of address used around Britain:

guv(ner)   from 'governor', an informal yet respectful term of address for an owner or boss, but may be used with irony

love   a term of casual or friendly address. A shopkeeper might say 'That'll be two pounds for the bread and milk, please love.' It's commonly used when speaking to members of the opposite sex, or between women, and is not flirtatious or impudent. Only in a few parts of England do men call each other *love*, instead of *mate* or *pal*. In Bristol and the southwest, the term *lover* or *old lover* is sometimes used, as in 'How are you, me old lover?' Once again, this is not flirtatious, nor a reference to a former romantic relationship.

master   once widely used in northern England, a polite yet informal variation of *Mister* or *Sir* (eg *Hast thou got bread in't shop today, master?* meaning 'Have you got bread in the shop today, mister?'). Occasionally used when addressing male children, usually humorously.

mate   used in casual address, as in 'Hey, mate, can you move your van?' The term is not restricted to men.

TITLES FOR TITLES

Just in case you're ever invited to tea with the Queen, or find yourself *hob-nobbing* with high-borns, here are the correct terms of address to use:

Your Majesty	the king or queen
Your Royal Highness	the monarch's spouse, children, sisters and brothers
Your Highness	the monarch's nephews, nieces and cousins
Your Grace	a duke or duchess (also an Anglican archbishop)
Lord/Lady	those below the rank of duke/duchess (ie Marquis/Marchioness, Earl/Countess, Viscount/Viscountess, Baron/Baroness)

PLEASE & THANK YOU

Compared to English-speakers from other countries, the British can appear somewhat overzealous in the use of *please*. Elsewhere, a sign in a shop would read 'Pay Here' – in Britain, it's 'Please Pay Here'. Cashiers, after ringing up your items, will always state the amount you owe followed by the word *please*, as in 'Two pounds, please', even if you already know how much you owe and are extending it to them in your hand. They aren't being rude or unobservant, just stating the amount, and the *please* automatically comes with it.

It's the same with *thank you*. It would appear that many Brits simply can't say it too often. In less formal situations you'll hear *ta* (pronounced 'tar' or 'tah') or *cheers* instead of *thank you*.

SEE THE SIGNS

Despite the overuse of *please*, the British can appear brusque or proscriptive: there are signs everywhere. On public transport alone you'll encounter:

- *Do Not Alight While Bus is in Motion*
- *Do Not Speak to the Driver*
- *Mind the Gap*
- *No Standing on Upper Deck*
- *Passengers Must Have a Valid Ticket to Travel on this Bus*
- *Please Have Exact Change*
- *Pushchairs Must be Folded*
- *Stand on the Left*

In contrast, some signs are overly polite, such as *Kindly Refrain From Smoking* or *The Management Respectfully Requests That Guests Do Not Take Visitors To Their Rooms*. Others are long-winded. When you discover your hotel is in the throes of full-scale renovation, the explanatory sign won't say anything as simple as *Sorry for the Mess*, but rather *The Management Would Like To Apologise For Any Inconvenience Caused* – suggesting that they'd *like* to apologise but might not actually do it.

Etiquette

SORRY?

As well as being used in apologies, the word *sorry* is used to mean 'What did you say?' – in the same way as you might say 'Pardon?' or 'Excuse me?' You'll also normally hear *Sorry* in Britain instead of 'Pardon me' or 'Excuse me' when someone needs to get past you (in the street or a cinema, for example).

READING BETWEEN THE LINES

In British English, as in some other languages, opening phrases are not always as they appear. Below are some common phrases, and their more honest translations.

Far be it from me to say, but ...
   I'm determined you'll hear my opinion.
With all due respect ...
   I have no respect for your view.
No offence intended ...
   This may offend you, but I don't care.

TELEPHONE

Here are some translated British English telephone terms to help you avoid possible confusion:

directory enquiries   telephone information service

engaged   this means the line is occupied, or 'busy'. People don't use the term 'busy signal'; they simply say 'I can't get through, the line's engaged.'

ex-directory   unlisted number

ring   the British *ring* (or *ring up*) people, rather than 'call' them (eg 'I'll ring you tonight')

Who is that?   the equivalent of 'Who's there?' or 'Who's calling?' (note, not 'Who's this?' as in American and Australian English)

ON THE BLOWER

A slang term for the phone is the *blower*, which harks back to the days when telephone mouthpieces were shaped like a horn. In London and the South, you might *get on the dog* to make a call. No animal cruelty is involved: it's short for *dog and bone* – Cockney rhyming slang for 'phone' (see pages 166–70 for more).

Weather

In Britain the weather is notoriously changeable – it can be warm and sunny in the morning then snowing by lunchtime – so it's a constant source of conversation. In towns and cities, in the rare cases that Brits speak to strangers chances are it'll be about the weather. They might say, 'It's cold today, isn't it?' or 'I wonder if this rain will ever stop, don't you?'

In the countryside a casual nod or quick hello in passing is not unusual even between strangers, but once again any other conversation is likely to be about the weather.

The Brits never seem to be happier than when complaining about the weather. If it's not too wet, it's too dry, and if it's not too hot, it's too cold. Even when conditions are incontestably beautiful, a common response to a cheery 'Lovely day, isn't it?' is 'Can't last though.' Some other weather-related terms include:

cutting	very cold ('That wind is cutting' – used in eastern England)
drizzle	light rain
fret	sea mist (in northeast England)
lashing	raining heavily ('It's lashing down.')
mizzle	a mix of light rain and mist
muggy	humid
pitching	settling ('The snow is pitching, not melting away' – southwest England)

raining cats and dogs	raining hard
scorcher	a hot day (a traditional British tabloid headline in August is 'Phew, What a Scorcher!')

INTERROGATIVE, ISN'T IT?

When conversing with the locals, be ready for the quintessentially British expressions *isn't it?* and *didn't it?* (or *didn't she?*, *isn't he?*, *didn't they?* and so on). These are tacked on to the end of a surprisingly large number of statements – turning them unexpectedly into questions. It can be confusing for foreigners.

In Britain, when people give an opinion, it sounds like they won't allow the listener to be noncommittal: 'Sarah's behaviour is outrageous, isn't it?'

Even more disconcerting is the British habit of (apparently) seeking corroboration on things you couldn't possibly know: 'I had a date with Steve last night, and I spilled a drink all over him, didn't I?' The custom reaches new heights when used as a snappish retort. Friends might say: 'John, we've been waiting for an hour.' John's annoyed reply: 'I was stuck in traffic, wasn't I?'

These aren't real questions. The trick when replying to one is to focus on the main statement, and reply as usual – 'Oh, really' or 'Oh no, what a shame', as appropriate. If in doubt, remember the golden rule: it's not really a question, is it?

At home, at work or at school, on the town or in the country, there are a host of British English words and phrases that might not be understood by English speakers from abroad. This chapter will guide you through some of the essentials.

Home

TYPES OF DWELLING

It's not a big place, so Britain can seem crowded at times, with the inhabitants living *cheek by jowl* (close to one another) in *flats*, *bedsits* or *semis*. If those words don't confuse you, there are many others which might! Below is a selection of terms to describe homes and houses, and the rooms within them.

bedsit short for *bedsitting room*, literally a single room for living and sleeping, usually in a large house converted into several bedsits. A byword for any small basic rented accommodation.

bungalow any single-storey house

council house house built by a town or city council, often with subsidised rent

detached house a free-standing house (not joined to any other). The word is generally used in an urban environment. A lonely cottage in the country would not usually be referred to as a detached house.

digs colloquial term for lodgings or a place to stay (usually short term)

estate a large area of land held by one person or family. See also **housing estate**.

flat dwelling in part of a larger building, usually larger than a **bedsit**, and usually – but not always – on one level. Called an 'apartment' in the US. The larger building usually contains many other flats or bedsits. A very large building containing many flats is called a **block of flats** (same as an 'apartment block' in the US).

housing estate group of houses, from a few to several hundred, planned and built by a town council or private developer. On some housing estates, new schools, shops and community facilities are also built.

maisonette when a large house is divided into two (or more) separate dwellings, one on each floor, the term **maisonette** is sometimes used instead of **flat**

semi-detached house two houses joined by a common wall, but otherwise standing alone (often shortened to **semi**)

studio flat euphemism for **bedsit**, or sometimes for a smarter bedsit (some Brits wryly say that a studio flat is a bedsit that you can't afford)

terraced houses row of houses, usually all built to the same plan and attached to one another

BEDSIT LAND – MY ONLY HOME

An area of a large city with a concentration of rented rooms is known as **bedsit land**. With the term come implications of loneliness, single life, anonymity and a temporary existence. The melancholy Morrissey of The Smiths was known by some as the **Bard of Bedsit** – also a title given to the equally downbeat Leonard Cohen. (Morrissey was also known as the **Mancunian Misanthrope** and the **Pope of Mope**. How the Brits love wordplay!)

AROUND THE HOUSE

Visitors from overseas may find familiar objects with very unfamiliar names inside the typical British house. (For terms used in specific regions, see the Regional Variations chapter.)

bath what Americans call 'the bathtub'. Where the British might say 'He's in the bath', Americans would say 'He's in the tub.'

bin where the household *rubbish* ('trash' to Americans) goes, usually indoors (eg 'Put it in the bin under the sink'). *Bin* is often used as a verb: 'Bin it' means 'Throw it away.'

cling film transparent food wrap; called 'Saran Wrap' or 'cellophane' in US English and 'Glad Wrap' or 'cling wrap' in Australian English

clothespeg clip for holding washed clothes to a line; called a 'clothes-pin' in the US

curtain rails plastic or metal rods from which curtains hang

cutlery eating utensils such as knives and forks; 'silverware' in the US

dishcloth in British English, this is the small cloth used for doing the *washing up*; it's called a 'dishrag' in US English. The larger cloth used for drying clean dishes is called a *tea towel* in British English (and a 'dishcloth' in US English).

double glazing windows consisting of two layers of glass to insulate against cold and damp. Neither pane is removable.

dustbin large receptacle for rubbish, usually kept outside; called a 'garbage bin' or 'trash can' in the US

duvet (pronounced 'doovay') a warm quilt covering a bed, with a removable (washable) cover, meaning no top sheets or blankets are required. Called a 'doona' in Australian English, and sometimes called a 'comforter' in US English. If it lies on top of sheets and blankets and doesn't have a removable cover then it's called a *quilt* or *eiderdown* in British English.

en suite   bathroom attached to a bedroom. Some larger houses have one or more bedrooms with an en suite bathroom, as well as a bathroom that the whole family might share.

flannel   cloth used to wash your body, especially hands and face; 'washcloth' in the US

garden   outside area belonging to the house, usually with a lawn, or perhaps flower beds and a vegetable patch. The US equivalent is 'yard'. Some British houses have a **front garden** and a **back garden**.

grill   'to grill' means to cook under electric coils or a gas flame. *The grill* is usually in or above the oven. It's called a 'broiler' in US English. What Americans call 'the grill' (the cooker in the back yard) is called a **barbeque** in British English.

hedge   line of bushes grown around a garden to act as a barrier. Compare with **hedgerow** (page 59).

immersion heater   domestic (electric) hot water heater

jug   receptacle for carrying or pouring liquids; 'pitcher' in the US. (*Jugs* is also vulgar slang for breasts.)

kettle   receptacle used for boiling water to make tea or coffee. Occasionally called a **tea kettle**. The British don't use the word **kettle** to mean any pot or pan, apart from *fish kettle* (a saucepan for cooking fish) and, unexpectedly, *paint kettle* (a small pot for paint decanted from a larger container, used especially by professional house painters).

lodger   a person who rents one room in a house that's otherwise owned and occupied by someone else

lounge   living room; sitting room

skip   large metal receptacle for carrying away rubbish (after building work, for example); sometimes called a 'dumpster' in US English

tap   device for turning water on and off; called a 'faucet' or 'spigot' in the US

tenant a person who rents a house or apartment (when the house owner usually lives elsewhere)

wardrobe what Americans call a 'clothes closet'. This can be a moveable piece of furniture or 'built-in'.

washing up dirty dishes. People might say, for example 'Look at that pile of washing up in the sink' or 'You can't watch TV until you've done the washing up.'

waste bin small bin or basket in a kitchen or other room for small items of rubbish (if it's a genuine basket, sometimes called a ***wastebasket***)

wheelie bin outdoor rubbish bin on wheels

wireless old-fashioned term for a household radio

yard area outside (and usually behind) a house, probably concrete-covered, where cars may be parked or equipment stored

---

TOILET TROUBLE

The ***toilet*** in British English is also called the ***lavatory*** or ***WC*** – although both those terms are pretty dated. It's perfectly acceptable (even preferable in some circles) to call it the ***loo***.

Toilet means both the actual object (so a plumber might 'fit a new toilet') and the room (so you might 'leave the table to visit the toilet'). In Britain, people don't use the euphemism 'bathroom'. These days advertisers come right out and sell you ***toilet paper***, not 'bathroom tissue', too.

In pubs and restaurants you'll see signs for ***Ladies*** and ***Gents***. The many less charming British slang terms for the toilet include the ***bog*** and the ***lavvy***. The equivalent of the Aussie 'dunny' (ie a toilet in a separate building in the garden rather than in the house) is ***privy***. US terms such as 'john' or the 'can' are rarely used.

As to the action, while Americans speak of having to 'pee', the British are more likely to ***wee***.

Family

Parents in Britain are usually known as *mum* and *dad* (or *mummy* and *daddy* by young children, and by daughters of any age in well-to-do families). Note the spelling. It's not 'mom' and 'mommy' as in the US.

Grandparents are usually called *grandad* or *grandpa* and *grandma* or *granny* (or simply *gran*). Another common term for grandmother is *nan* or *nana* – the latter favoured by young children.

Auntie is the diminutive of *aunt* used by young children. *Uncle* remains *uncle*. Both terms are sometimes given by children to adult friends of their parent/s, even if there's no blood relationship.

Some other family-related words are:

baby-sitting informal or occasional arrangement, where a *baby-sitter* (usually a family friend or relative) looks after children in the evening while the parents are out. Not the same as a *child-minder*.

bairn baby (in northern England and Scotland)

buggy/pushchair small chair on wheels (usually folding) for children; called a 'stroller' in the US. A *pushchair* generally means the bigger version used for small children; a *buggy* is lighter.

child-minder someone who looks after children during the day, usually on a regular (paid) basis at their own home or the home of the children (while the parent/s are at work). This term is generally not applied to employees at a *crèche* or *nursery* (see definitions following).

cot small bed specifically for a baby or young child; called a 'crib' in US English

crèche place that looks after babies and pre-school children while their parents are at work, usually attached to the place of work. Also found at some supermarkets and other very large shops, health clubs and so on.

cuddly toy stuffed toy animal

dummy plastic and rubber or silicone, often teat-shaped, given to babies to suck or chew; called a 'pacifier' in the US

nursery a place that looks after babies and pre-school children on a regular basis. Sometimes informally called a *play-school* and formally called a *pre-school* when it's for children around three to four years old – about a year before they go to 'proper' primary school (see the Education section, following). The term *nursery* originally meant the room in a large house where the family's children would play. (The US equivalent is 'daycare', but this is rarely used in Britain in the context of children; it generally applies to a place where elderly or ill people are looked after.)

nappy absorbent underwear worn by non-toilet-trained children; called a 'diaper' in the US

pram effectively a small bed on wheels for babies that cannot yet sit up on their own in a *pushchair*. The word is a shortened form of *perambulator* – meaning 'something you can walk with'.

ON THE CARDS

The day some countries (including Britain) call *Mother's Day* is also known as *Mothering Sunday*. Originally a festival to honour Mary, mother of Jesus, it has now become an annual opportunity to send a card and bunch of flowers to your mum. The British version of this day is based on the church calendar, and is on the fourth Sunday in Lent.

Father's Day has no biblical origin – it was invented by a greeting card manufacturer simply to boost sales.

BRAND NAMES

Throughout Britain, these brand names have become either totally or partly synonymous with the generic product:

Domestos	liquid bleach
Durex	condom
Hoover	vacuum cleaner
Land Rover	all-terrain vehicle
Nescafé	instant coffee
Savlon	antiseptic ointment
Sellotape	transparent adhesive tape
TCP	antiseptic liquid
Tipp-ex	correction fluid
WD-40	fine lubricant in a spray can
Zimmer frame	walking aid, usually for old people

Education

There are regional variations but British education falls into three major stages:

primary school	for children aged around 5 to 11
secondary education	from around 11 years onward: obligatory to age 15 or 16, optional to age 18
tertiary education	for those over 18 – ie university or college

This section covers some main components of the education system in Britain – although in some cases they apply to England only. The education system in Wales is similar to England's, while Scotland has its own education system which differs in some areas.

There are many British English words and phrases to do with education which people from other English-speaking countries might not understand, so *sit up straight* and listen at the back, here are some guidelines:

A-levels   short for 'Advanced levels' – examinations which students aspiring to go to university take, usually at around age 18, as entrance qualifications

A-S-levels   exams taken a year before A-levels

college   a college may be part of a university (like one of the colleges of Oxford or Cambridge) or a stand-alone educational establishment, either for students 16 to 18 (also called 'sixth form college') or for those over 18 – for example a teacher-training college or a technical college. (The word, *college* is also used informally to mean university – you might hear a school-leaver say 'I'm going to college in Manchester next year' when they mean they're going to Manchester University. Interestingly, the term is rarely used this way by students heading for Oxford or Cambridge.)

comprehensive school   a type of secondary school that's publicly funded and requires no special qualifications to enter (unlike a grammar school)

form   a grade or level of progression in school. Usually used in *secondary education*. *Form one* (or *first form*) is the first year of secondary school, *form two* is the second year, and so on. Many schools now use the term *year* instead (*year one*, *year two*, *year three* etc). In American terms, *form one* is roughly sixth grade, *form two* is roughly seventh grade, and so on.

grammar school   a publicly funded secondary school that only pupils with a certain level of academic achievement can enter – usually pupils must pass a test at the end of primary school, officially titled (or in some places unofficially dubbed) the *11-plus exam*

GCSE   short for *General Certificate of Secondary Education*, the name for examinations taken by all 16-year-olds. GCSE results are shown to employers or used to gain entry to *sixth form colleges* where A-levels are studied.

lecturer   teacher at a university or **college** (the term **tutor** is also used). As well as teaching, most lecturers and tutors also do research, write papers and so on.

maths   short for **mathematics** (what Americans call 'math')

middle school   in most parts of Britain, children go to primary school then secondary school, switching over at about age 11. In some areas, however, they attend middle school (from about 9 to 13 years old) in between primary and secondary.

Oxbridge   the word for Oxford and Cambridge when speaking of the two universities together. A student joining one of these august institutions is said to be **going up to** Oxford or Cambridge.

professor   a senior academic at a university, engaged in teaching, research and administrative duties. Each department within the university usually has only one professor – effectively he or she is the head of that department.

public school   a secondary school that (despite the name) is neither publicly funded nor open to the general public. A **public school** is a private or independent school, usually several centuries old, of high educational standard and costly to attend. Eton, Rugby, Harrow and Winchester are famous examples of public schools. (Many public schools are also charities, which gives them extra tax advantages.)

reader   university lecturer of high academic ranking in both teaching and research

revise   to study or prepare for an exam. Thus, when British students talk about **revising** they don't mean rewriting a paper, they mean studying (as in 'I have to stay in tonight and revise for my biology exam').

supply teacher   substitute or temporary teacher, filling in for the usual teacher who is on sick leave or study leave

swot   a slang term meaning to study intensively for an examination. ('I stayed up all night to swot for my exams.')

The US equivalent is 'cram'. In British English a pupil who studies regularly might be called *a swot* disapprovingly by classmates.

tuition   this word has several meanings: teaching, tutoring, and lessons (whether private or class). Hence, *tuition fees* – the money students pay for their tertiary education.

Work

Some job titles in British English are not the same as in other parts of the English-speaking world.

barrister   a lawyer who argues cases in court (a *solicitor*, by contrast, prepares the client's case out of court)

caretaker   what Americans call a 'janitor'

charlady   old-fashioned term for a female cleaner

collier   coal miner

dustman   garbage collector

farrier   blacksmith who shoes horses

gaffer   slang term meaning boss or foreman (possibly derived from Arabic *gaffier*, meaning 'guardian')

GP   General Practitioner – a family doctor as opposed to a specialist or hospital doctor

news agency   a news organisation like Reuters

newsagent   both a person who works in a small newspaper shop and the shop itself

lollipop lady/man a guard at road crossings near schools, to stop traffic when children cross. The name comes from the large sign they carry to warn vehicles.

postman a man who collects or delivers the post (ie the mail). Although many postal workers are female, the term 'postman' is proving hard to shake – perhaps thanks partly to children's cartoon character Postman Pat.

POST HASTE

In Britain, a ***post box*** (mail box) is where you ***post your letters***. When the postman delivers your mail, it comes through the ***letterbox*** – usually not a box at all, but a slot in the front door.

publican owner or manager of a pub. Also called a ***landlord***, irrespective of their actual ownership position.

sister senior nurse on a hospital ward (also called a ***matron***, although neither term is officially used any longer: ***nurse manager*** or a similar term is preferred)

solicitor see ***barrister***. (Note that the sign 'No Solicitors', which you might see on office doors in America, is not used in Britain. The British equivalent is ***No Hawkers*** or ***No Visitors Without an Appointment***.)

turf accountant a term used to describe a person who works at a betting shop – where you go to stake money on a horse race. (It's also a name for the betting shop itself.) The term may have been coined originally as a euphemism, but it's now a formal term – although not used so commonly these days.

vicar clergyman in the Anglican Church (Church of England)

OFFICE JARGON

In Britain, as elsewhere, office workers – and especially managers – have developed their own terminology; many of the British words are derived from American corporate-speak. Here are some favourites used in British English:

big ask   tough or demanding ('This job has to be finished next week. It's a big ask, but everyone will have to work over the weekend.')

ducks in a row   organised ('We're falling behind and really need our ducks in a row on this job'). Not to be confused with ***cocks on the block*** – meaning it's a major risk and there'll be serious damage if it fails.

face time   a meeting or discussion in person, as opposed to on the phone

going forward   in the future – much loved in office-speak. Mangled variations include 'in terms of going forward' and even 'going forward-wise'.

legs   feasibility ('The plans look good, but has this project got legs?'). Other variations are ***will it run?*** and ***will it fly?*** If a plan seems unfeasible a sceptic might say 'It'll never fly.'

park   to set aside a topic to be discussed later, so that the meeting or discussion can focus on the main issue. Variations are 'put it in long-term parking' or 'park it nearby, and keep the engine on'.

to go pear-shaped   to have problems; to fail ('Things were going well, then the finance collapsed and it all went pear-shaped.')

TURNING ON THE AGONY

It's not a job that lots of people do, but it's a job that influences the actions of a vast section of society: an *agony aunt* is the writer of an advice column in a magazine – usually she responds to reader queries about relationship and lifestyle issues. The US equivalent is 'Dear Abby'.

Love & dating

The term 'dating' is not commonly used in Britain. People might *go on a date*, but once it gets regular the term *seeing* or *going out with* is used instead. An example: 'I've been going out with a girl, her name is Julie.' Sometimes the old-fashioned term *courting* is used ironically – when the courting (in the sense of trying to win affection) is over, and the relationship is happening. Here are some other British love and dating terms you may encounter:

chat up   to attempt to endear oneself. The US equivalent is 'come on to' or 'hit on'. For example: 'I was in this bar, and this lovely guy tried to chat me up.' A *chat-up line* is a 'smooth' opening line, the classic being 'Haven't I seen you somewhere before?' In Britain, being *chatted up* is okay, if you like the person who's doing the chatting up. It's not used as a derogatory or scathing term, as it might be in some other forms of English – well, not always.

cop off   to meet someone, usually at a party or similar, and end the evening with sexual activity

crumpet   attractive woman (the term is generally used by men). Also used as a plural: 'The lads were on the town, looking to pull crumpet.'

have it off   slightly vulgar and immature way of describing sex ('They'd only just been introduced, but two hours later they were having it off in the back of a car.')

playing away   having an extra-marital affair

pull   When used as a verb, *pull* has a similar meaning as *cop off*. It can also be used as a noun; someone might be described as *a great pull*. Another version is *on the pull*, ie looking for a romantic or sexual encounter.

quickie   this originally meant anything done quickly or in a hurry; it now means quick sex *randy*   slang term for feeling libidinous or aroused (also sometimes means 'arousing')

shag   vulgar slang for sex (as in 'I had a great shag last night'); also used to define a person's sexual prowess: 'I met this guy; he was a great shag.' Hence also *shagger* (someone who *shags* a lot, or aims to) and *shagging* (eg 'John and Jane were caught shagging in the bathroom'). *Shagged* is also slang for 'very tired'.

snog   a long kiss, especially in a teenage context. For example: 'John and Jane started the night having a snog in the broom-cupboard.' Also used as a verb: 'I'd really like to snog you.' Hence also *snogging*.

toy-boy   younger male lover

two-timing   having a relationship with two people at the same time (keeping each secret from the other)

Politics & government

The British Parliament calls itself the *Mother of Parliaments*, being one of the oldest in the world, and having exported its concepts to many other countries. Thus, some British terms relating to politics and government are also used in, say, India, Australia or the US. However, many other terms have remained unique to Britain. Here are some official and jargon terms that could be confusing if you're not familiar with British politics:

bill   a draft act of parliament, to be debated by *MPs* and members of the *House of Lords*. When a bill is *passed* it becomes an *act of Parliament*, and the basis for law.

cabinet   key decision-making body of government. Consists of the Prime Minister and ministers.

Chancellor of the Exchequer   Cabinet minister in charge of the national treasury (often called the 'Minister of Finance' in other countries). Not to be confused with the *Lord Chancellor*.

Conservative Party   right-of-centre political party, one of the two major parties in British politics. Also called the **Tory Party**.

dissemble   an obscure term which entered political jargon when an **MP** found himself unable to say he'd previously lied to his colleagues; instead he said he'd **dissembled** the facts. The term is now used on occasion by other **MPs**, as they are not allowed to accuse one another of lying during debates in the **House of Commons**. (If they do, they're evicted by the **Speaker**.)

Downing Street   a small street off a major thoroughfare in London called Whitehall. Number 10 Downing Street is the official residence of the Prime Minister, and Number 11 is the official residence of the Chancellor of the Exchequer. Hence **Downing Street** and **Number 10** are terms often used synonymously with 'the Government'.

Eurosceptic   a politician opposed to Britain's ties with the European Union

filibuster   to speak for an unnecessarily long period, to deliberately waste time so that a parliamentary debate ends without conclusion: effectively a technique for preventing a **bill** becoming an **act**

guillotine motion   a discussion in parliament for which there's only limited time

House of Commons   the lower house of Parliament, consisting of around 600 elected **Members of Parliament** (**MPs**)

House of Lords   the upper house of Parliament; currently an unelected body composed of nobles, appointed peers and high-ranking clergy

Labour Party   centre-left political party, one of the two major parties in British politics

Liberal Democrats   centrist party, third-strongest in Britain; often shortened to **Lib-Dems**

lobby   to *lobby* an MP is to speak with an MP in order to press a case or ask for support on a certain matter. The term originates from the place where MPs would meet petitioners (the 'central lobby' at Parliament is the main entrance hall).

Lord Chancellor   more formally called the **Lord High Chancellor**, the head of the judiciary and senior figure in the *House of Lords*

MP   abbreviation for *Member of Parliament* (ie a member of the *House of Commons*)

MSP   a Member of the Scottish Parliament

the Opposition   more formally called *Her/His Majesty's Loyal Opposition*, this refers to the principal party opposing the governing party in the British Parliament

Prime Minister   the head of the government, usually the leader of the party holding the majority of seats in the *House of Commons*. (There are not separate elections for the Prime Minister in Britain, as there are for presidents and other heads of state in some other countries – the British head of state is the monarch.)

quango   acronym for 'quasi-autonomous non-governmental organisation': a semi-public administrative body, outside the Civil Service but receiving financial support from the government. The senior members of a *quango* are appointed by the government.

reshuffle   an interchange of posts among government ministers, which occurs every year or so

Secretary of State   minister who heads a major government ministry such as Education or Health

HOUSE OF HISTORY

The British Parliament is derived from the English Parliament that was formed during the 13th century from the great councils of the Plantagenet kings. The origin of the word 'parliament' goes back even further. Early written histories mention William the Conqueror and his advisors having 'very deep speech' – *parlement* in the Conqueror's Norman French.

In the 14th century Parliament assumed the right to make laws and control taxation, and the division into the Houses of Lords and Commons became permanent.

During the 18th century, the Cabinet and the office of Prime Minister developed, and in 1911 the *Parliament Act* limited the power of the House of Lords, finally giving legislative supremacy to the Commons.

Today, Parliament's term is a maximum of five years, but a government may call a general election earlier if it chooses.

---

shadow minister a member of the main opposition party who focuses on certain issues. So the Shadow Health Minister would concentrate on health matters, the Shadow Chancellor on finance matters, and so on. The *Leader of the Opposition* and the shadow ministers together form the *shadow cabinet*.

silly season the late-summer period when Parliament is in recess, when newspapers publish stories about trivial matters

Speaker key figure in the *House of Commons*; the *Speaker* keeps order during debates, calls on *MPs* to make speeches and casts the deciding vote in the case of ties

spin a shorthand term for a message from the government where positives are emphasised or negatives hidden, and by extension for political manipulation of the media. Lazy journalists imply that *spin* is a modern phenomenon, but rulers and governments have engaged in *spin* since the days of Ancient Egypt – and possibly longer. The word has now entered mainstream vocabulary – a company director may be accused by shareholders of *spinning* a report on lacklustre financial results, for example.

surgery   place where an *MP* meets his or her constituents one-to-one – usually at the MP's local office

Westminster   the formal name for the Houses of Parliament in London is the 'Palace of Westminster', and so the term *Westminster* is also used to refer to Parliament. (The Palace of Westminster is in the City of Westminster, a separate city within London.)

Whitehall   major street in London where many ministries and government offices are located

Town & country

Britain is, as the brochures say, a land of contrasts. In between the towns and cities are large areas of open countryside. Well, they're large by British standards, although visitors used to the Outback or Alaska may not agree …

TOWN

Most urban settlements in Britain are towns. In fact the name comes from *tun*, an Old English term meaning 'an enclosed or fortified village', remembered today by the numerous place names ending in *-ton* – Southampton, Workington, Weston and so on. Today in Britain a town can have anything from several hundred inhabitants to several thousand. Essentially, it's larger than a village and smaller than a city – although there are a few exceptions. This section covers some British phrases relating to towns and other urban areas.

borough an urban community (technically one that has been 'incorporated' by royal charter), either standing alone (many market towns across England are boroughs) or forming part of a city. (London has 32 boroughs.) The word is derived from the Old English word *burg* (meaning 'fortified town').

city a very large urban settlement, such as London, Manchester, Birmingham, Edinburgh, Glasgow or Cardiff. Generally, the British definition of a city differs from the American. British cities generally have several hundred thousand inhabitants (some have several million). Many places in the US called 'cities' would be called 'towns' in Britain.

The City the financial district of London: the British equivalent of Wall Street. The City is governed by the Lord Mayor – whose post is largely ceremonial, and quite separate from the Mayor of London (who is an elected official responsible for the entire metropolis of London).

city centre the central part of a city; the area known as 'downtown' or the 'central business district' in other English-speaking countries

close a street closed at one end, also called a *dead-end street*; also an enclosure or enclosed place, such as a precinct of a cathedral. Pronounced as in 'dose', not 'doze'. The word dates back to medieval England and originates from Old French *clos*.

common area of land, usually grassy, held in common ownership by all members of a community; sometimes the

---

SPOT THE CITY

Although most British cities are very large, the precise definition of a city is 'any settlement which has a cathedral'. This gives rise to a few anomalies; for example, the small Welsh town of St David's (population 1800) has a cathedral, and claims to be the smallest city in Britain.

HIGH TRADITION

The *high street* is a British institution, a long-standing tradition and, for many people, an object of some affection. Some see the typical British high street as part of the national heritage, and something to be protected against the rise of huge out-of-town shopping centres (what Americans call a 'mall') that attract thousands of customers and have already killed off high streets in many parts of the country.

common may be owned by an individual but others in the community still have right of access

high street the primary street or road in a town, where the bulk of the shops are – the butcher, the baker, the greengrocer, the newsagent, the chemist and so on. It's not the exact equivalent of US 'main street', but similar. See the box above for more.

the Met abbreviation for the London Metropolitan Police Department. (Not to be confused with the *Met Office*, which is short for the Meteorological Office – Britain's national weather service.)

mews dwellings grouped around an open yard or alley

minster alternative word for cathedral (as in York Minster). Hence *Westminster* – from West Minster – the original name of the great church built in the medieval period to the west of the original City of London, and now giving its name to the surrounding area.

pavement paved pedestrian walkway beside a road; 'sidewalk' in US English, 'footpath' in Australian English

village a rural settlement, usually of a few hundred inhabitants – smaller than a town. Some definitions state that a village must have a few facilities (such as a post office, pub, shop, church and primary school) but the term is used to mean 'any small settlement'. If a place is really small (just a few houses and maybe a church) it's called a *hamlet*.

MEWS DEVELOPMENT

The word *mews* has an interesting history. In medieval times, it referred to a set of cages for keeping hawks during moulting. Later, it designated the royal stables at Charing Cross in London, built on the site of the old royal hawk mews. Later still, it meant any set of stables grouped around an open yard or alley. Eventually, mews were converted into lodgings, and in the 19th century, rows of townhouses were actually built in the style of mews.

Today, living in a *mews house* is highly desirable, and new developments are still constructed in *mews style*. The word *mews* is also a designation for an address, and you'll find it on street maps just like 'street' or 'road': *Glynde Mews* or *Halkin Mews* in London, for example.

COUNTRY

Many countries are identified with a particular natural or man-made topographical feature – think of Russia's steppes, America's prairies or Holland's dykes and canals. Britain also has its special features; here's a small selection:

barrow   prehistoric burial mound. Numerous *barrows* exist in Britain, many dating from the Bronze Age.

bridleway   path originally for horse-riders, but which can also used by walkers and cyclists

broad   low-lying lake (in east England). *The Broads* is an area of wetlands in the county of Norfolk in eastern England.

dale   valley, usually small or medium-sized, often in the chalk-land or limestone areas of northern England

downs   treeless, grass-covered undulating hills, usually on chalk soil, especially in southern England; also called *down-lands*. (No, you didn't misread – the downlands are uplands.)

earthwork   prehistoric fortification – often a circular or rectangular embankment made of earth, frequently the subject of archaeological studies

fen low, marshy area of land. *The Fens* is a formerly marshy area of eastern England, now drained by a network of canals and ditches (many called *dykes*) and a rich farming area.

firth river estuary, such as the *Firth of Forth* and the *Firth of Clyde* in Scotland. The word is related to the Norse word fjord.

footpath path for walkers or hikers in a rural area, or a path in an urban area that doesn't run along the roadside. Many are *rights of way* – see the box on page 60.

gorse bush with sharp thick spines and small yellow flowers that grows on heath and other sandy areas. Also known as *furze*.

heath tract of open land, generally covered with low, patchy shrubs such as *broom* or *gorse*; also called *heathland*

hedgerow very large hedge containing numerous different species of tree and bush, and forming a barrier around farmland – effectively a natural wall or fence. The hedgerows of Britain are notable for their size: they're often one to two metres wide and the same height or higher, and stretch unbroken for miles between farmers' fields and between fields and roads in cultivated areas.

market town in the medieval period, towns depended on trade to prosper and grow, but had to gain permission from the monarch, in the form of a royal charter, to hold regular markets. Those that did were designated *market towns*. Today it's a term for any medium-sized town, usually one that has existed for a few centuries at least.

BARROW BOY

If you've read Thomas Hardy's *The Return of the Native*, you'll remember Rainbarrow, a burial mound which figures prominently in the novel. It protrudes from a section of heathland near Hardy's childhood home in Dorset.

mead low-lying field or meadow, usually near a river

moor area of high open land with dark peaty soil, usually devoid of trees and covered in rough grass and plants such as heather. Emily Brontë's *Wuthering Heights* is set on the moors of West Yorkshire, near Haworth.

plantation in Britain, this an area planted with trees, particularly conifers (rather than, say, bananas or cotton)

wold hill, as in the Yorkshire Wolds, Lincolnshire Wolds and the Cotswolds (which is where you find the market town of Stow-on-the-Wold)

GO THE RIGHT WAY

Perhaps because Britain is such a crowded place, open spaces are highly valued, and every weekend millions of Britons get their boots on and take to the countryside. Every town and village is surrounded by a web of footpaths, while most patches of open land are crossed by paths and tracks.

The joy of walking in Britain is due in no small part to the *right of way* network – public paths and tracks across private property. Nearly all land in Britain is privately owned (including land within national parks), but if there's a right of way, you can follow it through fields, woods, even farmhouse yards, as long as you keep to the route and do no damage. Some mountain and moorland areas of England and Wales are **Open Access Areas**, where walkers can move freely beyond rights of way (signboards or maps indicate when this is permitted). Scotland has a different system, with fewer actual rights of way, but a tradition of relatively free access in mountain and moorland areas – although there are restrictions during the grouse- and deer-hunting seasons.

The main types of right of way are *footpaths* and *bridleways* (the latter open to horse-riders and mountain-bikers too). There are also *byways*, unsurfaced tracks which due to a quirk of history are open to *all* traffic. This means walkers can be disturbed by off-road driving fanatics – a cause of considerable controversy in some areas.

There's a host of options for getting around Britain – whether by public transport or with your own set of wheels.

Driving

There are five main types of road in Britain: first, the **motorways**, the high-speed routes that go from city to city. The equivalents in other English-speaking countries are 'freeways' or 'inter-states'. British **motorways** are identified by numbers, like the **M1** (London to Leeds) and the **M5** (London to South Wales). Next are the **A-roads**, the main highways after motorways, and **B-roads**, smaller, narrower roads, though often still quite busy. Then come the **C-roads**, more often just called **lanes** or **country roads**, and last are the **unclassified roads** found in remote or rural areas, still tarred but often only wide enough for one car. These are also often called **lanes** – or **really narrow lanes** to distinguish them from the wider sort! Note that in Britain, the term **street** always means a road in a town or city.

THE NEED FOR SPEED

Most British drivers tend to **speed** (ie go faster than the legal limit). The presence of **speed traps** (police with radar guns) and **speed cameras** (automatic detection cameras, often called *Gatzos* – a brand name now used generically) doesn't have much impact. Even being stopped by the police and **done for speeding** (fined) doesn't seem to be a deterrent.

Driving

Whether driving down the road or up the street, here are some British terms to do with motor vehicles and the places they go:

articulated lorry   large truck with a cab and separate trailer attached by a joint. Often called a 'semitrailer' (or 'semi') elsewhere.

bonnet   the hinged panel at the front of the car, covering the engine. Called the 'hood' in the US.

boot   the storage space at the back of the car, where you put your bags. The 'trunk' in the US.

caravan   a 'house' on wheels, towed behind a car, usually for holiday purposes. (It has nothing to do with a chain of camels, but that's the derivation of the term.) Caravans are often called 'trailers' in US English, although that can refer to anything towed behind a car. In British English, very big caravans are called **mobile homes** – ironic since they're often so big they're not really mobile. These are also called **static caravans** or simply **statics**.

car park   the place where you park your car, called a 'parking lot' in the US. A **multi-storey car park** is what Americans might call a 'parking garage'.

central reservation   a length of concrete or grass dividing the traffic going in opposite directions on a multi-lane highway (nothing to do with an area for indigenous inhabitants). Called a 'median strip' in US and Australian English.

circus   an open space or intersection in a city, usually circular, with several streets converging on it (such as Piccadilly Circus in London and Colmore Circus in Birmingham)

diversion   detour (eg because the road is being repaired)

dual carriageway   a major road with at least two lanes of traffic in each direction, separated by a **central reservation** and usually a safety barrier

filter a term applied when traffic leaves the main highway. Hence, on a multi-lane road, the lane allowing you to slow down and turn off is called the **filter lane**. (A green arrow at a traffic light for turning lanes is sometimes called a **filter light**.) **Filter** is also a verb; your passenger may say, for example, 'You need to filter here.'

full beam see **high beam**

gearstick device for changing gears in a car – known to Americans as a 'gearshift' or 'stickshift'

handbrake what Americans call the 'emergency brake' or 'parking brake'

high beam headlights usually have two settings: **high beam** points straight ahead; **dipped** is when the light is dimmed to avoid dazzling on-coming drivers. The extra-strong headlights used on dark country roads at night or during bad weather at any time are called **foglights** or **spotlights**.

indicators flashing lights used to inform other drivers that you intend to turn; 'blinkers' in US English

island there are two sorts: **pedestrian islands**, which are safe halfway points for pedestrians crossing the road (officially called **pedestrian refuges**); and **traffic islands**, which are also known as **roundabouts** (see the next page)

junction the point at which any two roads meet or cross; also a point where it's possible to leave or join a motorway – what might be called an 'off-ramp' or 'on-ramp' elsewhere

lay-by a parking place at the side of a main road, usually with no facilities other than an overflowing rubbish bin (compare with **services**)

lorry a large goods vehicle – usually called a 'truck' elsewhere, although that term is used in Britain too

mudguard a wheel-cover on a motorbike or bicycle designed to protect the rider from road spray. In US English, a 'fender'.

pelican crossing   road crossing with pedestrian-activated traffic lights. 'Pelican' is a tortured acronym of 'Pedestrian Light-Controlled'.

petrol   fuel for cars; 'gasoline' in the US

roundabout   an intersection where traffic moves around a raised circular area or 'island'

services   a place where you can turn off the motorway to stop, rest, put petrol in your car, get something to eat, and so on. (For example: 'I'm dying for the loo, how far is it to the next services?')

slip road   a lane for accelerating or decelerating when joining or leaving a busy multi-lane highway such as a motorway

subway   an underground pedestrian passage used to get from one side of a road to the other. Not a place where underground trains run, as in New York, for example.

Tarmac   the term **Tarmac road** is used to mean any road surfaced in asphalt (as opposed to concrete). Originally written 'Tar-Mac', the second part of this term is derived from the name of a 19th-century British road-building engineer called John McAdam. Contrary to popular belief, McAdam did not introduce the use of tar – his 'McAdamised' (or 'Macadamised') roads were built from layers of stone. Tar was introduced in the early 20th century to keep dust down and hold the stones together, and the term 'Tar-Macadamised' was introduced, later being shortened to its present form.

tyre   British spelling of US 'tire'

verge   the strip on the side of the road; called the 'shoulder' in US and Australian English. In Britain, a verge is usually grassy or covered in gravel, and is occasionally called a **soft shoulder**. The term **hard shoulder** is used for the wide strip of tar on the edge of motorways and some other major roads, sometimes called the **emergency lane**. When motorways are being repaired there will often be a sign saying 'Traffic Use Hard Shoulder'.

wheel arch/wing   the metal piece of a car's body that goes over the wheel

windscreen   window at the front of a car; called a 'windshield' in the US

zebra crossing   pedestrian road crossing, marked by black and white stripes painted on the road – hence the name

Public transport

Britain's public transport is often derided by locals, but the bus and train networks can be a great way to get around. Note that it's always called ***public transport***, not 'public transportation' as in the US.

BUS

In Britain there's an important difference between a **bus**, which normally means a local bus, and a **coach**, which is normally a long-distance bus, often faster and more comfortable. In some towns and cities the **bus station** and the **coach station** are in different places, causing great confusion for visitors.

A few other terms include:

bus shelter   small building or some transparent plastic panels providing protection from the elements for passengers waiting at a bus stop

bus station   large building or area where many buses pass through or start/terminate their route

bus stop   a point on the road, usually marked by a sign, where a bus stops to pick up or set down passengers

double-decker   bus with two floors

Routemaster   the brand name of the original red London double-decker bus, regarded by many as an icon. The fleet was withdrawn in 2005 after many decades of service, despite a public campaign to keep them on the road.

TRAIN

There are two main sorts of train service on Britain's railways: **long-distance** or **inter-city** services; and **local** or **commuter** services. Here are some more rail-related terms:

booking office   place to buy tickets – especially for travel at a later date

buffet   a small café at a train station or on a train (where it's often called the **buffet car**)

Channel Tunnel   the tunnel under the English Channel which links Britain with France, through which high-speed trains carry passengers and vehicles. Occasionally dubbed the **Chunnel**.

level crossing   point where a road crosses a railway line on the same level (ie not via a bridge). The crossing is usually protected by gates which close when a train passes.

railway   generic term for the rail network; 'railroad' in the US

return ticket   a ticket which allows you to go to and come back from your destination

single ticket   a ticket for a one-way journey

standard class   the seating formerly known as 'second class'

trolley service   snacks and drinks available on the train on a trolley which is wheeled through the carriages by an attendant

the Tube   colloquial name for London's underground railway network

way out   exit

HAIL, TAXI

The Brits are typically reserved when hailing a taxi; they simply stick an arm out to be noticed by an on-coming taxi. Yelling 'Taxi!' is rather frowned upon.

Although the traditional **London cab** (also called **black cabs** or **black taxis**, despite the fact that they now come in a variety of colours) is not the cheapest way to get around London and other major cities, passengers can be sure of getting to their destination by the quickest possible route. To get a licence, London's **cabbies** (taxi drivers) must memorise thousands of streets, as well as the position of hotels, theatres, railway stations and a host of other locations. This font of expertise is known simply as **The Knowledge**.

Minicabs are freelance taxis that can only be hired by phone (not flagged down in the street), and are generally cheaper than **black cabs**. Drivers are not required to have **The Knowledge**, and passengers often find themselves having to give minicab drivers the most basic of directions.

Holidaying

A *holiday* means time off work or school – a 'vacation' in US English. People may say, for example, 'I'm taking a holiday in Spain this year' or 'I won't be at work next week – I'll be on holiday.'

Places to stay or visit on holiday include:

bed and breakfast   often shortened to *B&B*, this is essentially accommodation in a room (or rooms) in someone's house, and a truly great British institution

camp site   an area where tents can be pitched and caravans parked. Called a 'campground' or 'camping site' in some other English-speaking countries.

inn   technically, a *pub* with accommodation, but often loosely used to mean just a *pub* (see the Food & Drink chapter for more). It's a legal requirement in Britain for a place calling itself an *inn* to offer accommodation. That's why many pubs once called 'The Crown Inn' or 'The Oak Inn' are now called simply 'The Crown' or 'The Oak'.

seaside   an area, usually a resort, beside the sea. When Brits plan a holiday, they say they're going to the *seaside* rather than to 'the ocean', or simply 'the sea'. Even if the resort is on the Atlantic Ocean, it's still called the *seaside*.

theme park   a giant funfair with roller coasters and so on. What Americans would call an 'amusement park'.

Britain once boasted a cuisine so undesirable that it's no wonder there's no English equivalent of *Bon appétit*. Fortunately, these days it's easy to find decent food: for every **greasy spoon** and fast-food joint, there's a friendly pub or top-class restaurant with enticing specialities on the menu.

Having said that, Britain's culinary heritage of ready-sliced white bread, fatty meats and vegetables boiled to death (all washed down by tea with four sugars) remains firmly in place in many parts of the country. And that's before we get on to treats like **pork scratchings** and **deep-fried Mars bars**. (The latter was invented in Glasgow, so perhaps it's no surprise that Scotland, with help from high cigarette and alcohol consumption, has one of the worst rates of heart disease in Europe.)

The recent changes for the better in food in Britain are largely thanks to outside influences. Chinese and Indian restaurants have been around since the 1960s, of course, and are no longer considered exotic. It's quite usual for British people to cook a madras or vindaloo in their own home, whatever their cultural heritage. And out on the street, curry is the most popular takeaway food in Britain, outstripping even fish and chips.

FISH & CHIPS

All across Britain, fish and chips is a most popular meal – served in pubs and cafés, or available from takeaway shops (often known as **chippies**). Sometimes both the chips and the fish can be greasy and tasteless (especially once you get far from the sea), but good chips seem to go with good fish, so at towns with salt in the air this deep-fried delight is always worth trying. Fish and chips used to be the most popular takeaway in Britain, but in these multicultural times that accolade now goes to curry.

Food & drink

In more recent times Britain has seen the arrival of restaurants specialising in food from the Mediterranean region, Africa, the Caribbean, Japan, Thailand, Vietnam and many other countries. As a result, pastas, pizzas, tapas, moussaka, sushi, foo yung, baklava and other specialities are commonplace in restaurants, and even in everyday pubs and cafés.

The overall effect of these foreign influences has been the introduction of revolutionary ingredients (like crisp fresh vegetables), new condiments (like chilli or soy sauce), new techniques (like steaming) and new implements (like woks) to restaurants and kitchens across Britain. In the smarter eating houses, a mix of British food with cuisine from anywhere else is known as *fusion cooking*. In more modest environments, such as country pubs in the north of England, look out for crossover dishes like *Yorkshire pudding* filled with curry – a favourite that many would say epitomises British society today (see also the box on page 78).

Eating

Options for eating out in Britain are many and varied, but a good start is always a local *café* (usually pronounced 'caffy' and often shortened to *caff*). A British café can be a *greasy spoon* (a very straightforward snack bar where cleanliness isn't always top priority), or a smart and welcoming place with luxuries like napkins and tablecloths (sometimes called a *teashop*) – or it can be something in between.

Either way, a British café is not the same as a café in France or some other European countries. For a start, asking for Pernod may cause confusion, as most British cafés don't serve alcohol.

THE REGIONAL MEAL DIVIDE

In different areas of Britain, the term *dinner* can be used differently. In the south of England (and at any restaurant) it's a cooked evening meal. But in northern England it's the meal eaten around noon. Thus, factory workers in the south have a *lunch break*, while those in the north have a *dinner break*. The difference isn't always regional; it can be more of a class divide too – the posh folks say 'lunch', while the workers say 'dinner'.

The term *tea* is similarly divided. In the south it means a light meal or snack mid-afternoon. In the north, where *dinner* is eaten at noon, *tea* is the cooked meal in the evening.

If you happen to be making arrangements to meet someone in Britain, and they say 'Come round after dinner', it might be worth checking if this means 2pm or 8pm ...

Here are some other terms the Brits use when dining out:

bill   payment at a restaurant, at the end of the meal. You can ask for the *bill*, but not the 'check'. In Britain, a *cheque* is used to pay for goods or services, instead of using cash or credit card; it's the thing you tear out of your *chequebook*.

canteen   in British English this is a snack bar or refreshment room, usually found in places like factories, offices, schools, hospitals and military camps

dinner   a main meal. Depending on where you are in Britain, this can mean the main meal around midday or the main meal in the evening (see the box above).

tea   as well as the drink, *tea* can mean a meal in the evening (see the box above). It can also mean a light mid-afternoon meal consisting of cakes, sandwiches, scones or shortbread, served of course with a cup of tea. The term *high tea* is sometimes used for the latter variety, to distinguish it from 'normal' tea.

Eating

71

Typical British food

There are many ingredients and dishes unique to Britain, and even for the most globally recognisable items, visitors may have to deal with unusual names. A few are listed below.

Many of these words will be recognised by speakers of Australian, Canadian and New Zealand English (which share many similarities with modern British English), but may be more unusual to speakers of American English.

aubergine (pronounced 'ohberzheen' – the *g* sounds like the *s* in 'pleasure'). A large smooth-skinned purple vegetable, called an 'eggplant' in the US and Australia.

bacon in Britain this means a cut of pork, generally taken from the back of the pig, cured, smoked or salted, and thinly sliced. It's most commonly fried or grilled and eaten for breakfast or in a sandwich. It's often called 'Canadian Bacon' in America.

bangers colloquial term for sausages, often eaten with *mash* (mashed potato)

bannock Scottish speciality – a cross between a scone and a pancake

bap a large, wide, flat, soft bread roll

bara brith traditional Welsh spicy fruit loaf

beetroot red root vegetable; called a 'beet' in the US

biscuits this generally means sweet biscuits ('cookies' in the US). The terms *savoury biscuits*, *salted biscuits* or *cheese biscuits* are usually used for what Americans call 'crackers' (though the words *crackers* or *cream crackers* are also sometimes used in Britain).

bun bread roll, usually sweet – eg *currant bun*, *cream bun*

caster sugar usually for cooking, this is sugar with finer grains than the kind you'd put in your coffee, and more expensive

cawl (pronounced 'cow') traditional Welsh dish; a thick broth of mixed vegetables, or vegetables and meat

chips hot deep-fried potato pieces (called 'french fries' or 'fries' in the US) and traditionally eaten with fish in Britain (see the box on page 69)

clotted cream cream so heavy or rich that it's become almost solid (but not sour)

cornflour powder-fine maize flour; it's called 'cornstarch' in the US

courgette (pronounced 'cawzhet' – the *g* is pronounced like the *s* in 'measure'). A long thin green member of the gourd family. Called 'zucchini' in the US and Australia.

cream cracker white unsalted savoury biscuit

cream tea a special *tea* or *high tea* (see previous definitions) of *scones*, *clotted cream* and *jam*, served with a cup or pot of tea. This is known as a *Devonshire tea* in many English-speaking countries, but not in England (except of course in the county of Devon).

crisps thin slices of fried potato bought in a packet. Called 'potato chips', or just 'chips' in the US and Australia.

crumpet circular kind of bread, one side covered in small indentations, which is toasted and usually buttered lavishly before being eaten

double cream heavy or thick cream

HAM IT UP

In some parts of Britain, bacon is called *ham*, and so *cooked ham* describes the stuff you can eat straight away, as opposed to the stuff you have to grill or fry before slapping between two bits of bread.

Dundee cake fruit cake made with a particularly rich fruit mix and topped with almonds – a Scottish speciality but widely available in Britain

fishfinger strip of fish pieces covered in breadcrumbs, usually bought frozen and cooked by frying or grilling – a children's favourite

gammon thick slice of ham, in the sense of a 'ham steak' on a dinner menu, rather than a thin slice of breakfast ham (which is called **bacon** in most parts of Britain)

gateau (pronounced 'gatoh') a rich layer cake, especially one involving cream or fruit. The word was borrowed from French, and so the plural is **gateaux** (also pronounced 'gatoh'). Deliberately mispronouncing the word ('gatuks') is the basis for an old joke: 'A café charging £3 for a slice of gateaux? That's bollo.'

haggis traditional Scottish dish of ground meat or offal mixed with oatmeal, stuffed in a sheep's stomach or intestine, then baked. Originally a poor-man's sausage, it's now regarded as a delicacy in some areas. Some pubs and restaurants in Scotland serve very good **haggis**; it's also available deep-fried with **chips** at takeaways.

ice lolly in Britain this is flavoured ice on a stick

icing thick, sweet and solid covering on a cake; called 'frosting' in US English

icing sugar powdered sugar, used to make **icing**

jam fruit conserve. In US English 'jam' contains pieces of fruit, while 'jelly' has been strained. This distinction exists in British English, but the term **jam** is often used for the strained stuff as well.

jelly gelatine dessert, often poured into a mould to set; called 'Jell-O' in US English

joint cut of meat used for roasting

kipper smoked herring

laverbread a Welsh speciality that's not a bread at all, but cooked seaweed. It's traditionally served mixed up with oatmeal and bacon on toast – a very tasty combination.

lollipop/lollypop/lolly a *sweet* on a stick. If it's not on a stick, it's not a *lolly* (unlike in Australia). See the box on page 79 for more.

Marmite a dark and pungent yeast extract, usually spread on toast, that generations of Brits have either loved or hated from childhood. Similar to the Aussie favourite Vegemite, but not the same – oh no!

marrow a large, green-skinned, fleshy, edible gourd, sometimes called a 'squash' in the US (see also *squash*)

munchies a slang term used to mean 'hungry' (as in 'I've got the munchies'). It's especially used in the context of the deep desire for food resulting from serious drinking or the use of some recreational drugs – notably cannabis.

oatcakes sweet or savoury biscuits made from oats, either rough- or smooth-ground, and traditionally from Scotland. Served at breakfast in Scottish hotels or restaurants as an alternative to toast.

NAME THAT PASTY

The *Cornish pasty* – a mix of cooked vegetables wrapped in pastry – is now available everywhere in Britain, not just Cornwall. It's often available in meat varieties too, much to the chagrin of Cornish purists. Long before Tupperware, the pasty was an all-in-one lunch pack that tin miners could carry underground and leave on a ledge ready for mealtime. To avoid mixing pasties, each was marked with the owner's initials – always at one end, so the miner could eat half and safely leave the rest to snack on later, without it mistakenly disappearing into the mouth of a workmate.

Before going back to the surface, the miners traditionally left the last corner of the pasty as a gift for the spirits of the mine known as *knockers*, to ensure a safe shift next day.

pasty   (pronounced 'pastee' with an *a* as in 'apple') a half-moon-shaped savoury pastry, crimped along the curved side and filled with meat or vegetables. Its most famous form is the **Cornish pasty**.

pickle   a thick, vinegary vegetable-based condiment. Called 'relish' in US English. The British don't speak of 'a' **pickle** – one singular **pickle** – they speak of **pickle** as a substance, like soup or oatmeal. ('Would you like some pickle with your cheese?') When referring to single items, however, the specific name is used (for example, **pickled egg**, **pickled cucumber**, **pickled onion**).

pips   seeds found in fruit

plaice   a flat saltwater fish, a kind of flounder. It's frequently included on menus, usually de-boned, coated in batter (and sometimes breadcrumbs), deep-fried and served with **chips**.

ploughman's lunch   thick slices of bread and cheese, commonly served in pubs, now available in many varieties (see the box below)

PLOUGHMAN'S PROGRESS

The **ploughman's lunch** is a British speciality – especially in pubs. Although hearty yokels almost certainly did carry a lump of cheese and a lump of bread to the fields (possibly even wrapped in a red-spotted handkerchief) over many centuries, the name is a modern phenomenon. It was invented in the 1960s by the marketing chief of the national cheese-makers' organisation as a way to boost consumption, neatly cashing in on public nostalgia and a willingness to maintain tradition.

You can still find basic **ploughman's lunches**, but these days this meal has usually been smartened up to include butter, salad, pickle, pickled onion and dressings. At some pubs you get a selection of cheeses. You'll also find other variations – **farmer's lunch** (bread and chicken), **stockman's lunch** (bread and ham), **Frenchman's lunch** (brie and baguette) and **fisherman's lunch** (you guessed it, with fish).

pork scratchings   deep-fried chunks of pig skin and fat, often sold in packets in pubs. Heavy in calories, and an acquired taste.

porridge   called 'oatmeal' by North Americans

pudding   this can mean a sweet dessert such as *butterscotch* or *chocolate pudding*, or a type of cake (eg *Bakewell pudding*), or a savoury dish (like *steak and kidney pudding*). It's also a general word for 'dessert'.

pulses   general term for the edible seeds of leguminous plants, such as beans, peas and lentils

salad cream   creamy vinegary salad dressing, much sharper than mayonnaise

savoury   when used to describe flavour, this means 'not sweet', whether it's salty, herbal or sour. In other words, a dish is said to be either *sweet* or *savoury*.

scone   a small doughy bread, traditionally served with jam and cream. Pronounced either 'scon' (to rhyme with 'on') or 'scown' (to rhyme with 'own').

Scotch broth   a thick soup made with barley, lentils and mutton stock. Sometimes offered as a *starter* in restaurants, but filling enough as a meal in itself.

shepherd's pie   a two-layered oven dish with a ground beef and onion mixture on the bottom and mashed potato on the top. Though it's called a pie, there's no crust.

single cream   light cream (to distinguish from *double* or *clotted* cream – see definitions earlier)

sorbet   flavoured frozen dessert; called 'sherbet' in some countries

spotted dick   this sounds like an embarrassing disease, but it's really a dessert – suet pudding with currants and raisins

spring onion   small white onion with a long green stalk which is also edible, usually chopped and eaten raw in salads

PUDDING ON THE STYLE

Perhaps one of the best known of British puddings is *Yorkshire pudding*, made from a simple batter mix baked in the oven. It rises high, with a crisp crust around the edge. A dash of beer in the batter adds to the flavour. Alternatively, add sausages and you've got another British classic: *toad-in-the-hole*.

Black pudding is a large sausage made from ground meat, offal, fat and blood. Traditionally served sliced and fried for breakfast, it's known in other countries as 'blood sausage', but the British version has a high proportion of oatmeal and so doesn't melt apart in the pan when fried.

Moving on to something sweeter, *plum pudding* is a dome-shaped cake with fruit, nuts, and sometimes brandy or rum, eaten traditionally at Christmas and also known as *Christmas pudding*. It's steamed rather than baked, cut into slices, and served with brandy butter. Watch out for the small coins inserted by superstitious cooks – if you bite on one it means good luck for the following year, but may mean bad news for your teeth.

squash   a generic term for some varieties of edible gourd (eg *butternut squash*, *gem squash*)

starter   the first course of a meal (usually a soup or light dish), known as an *hors d'œuvre* in France, an *antipasto* in Italy, a *Vorspeise* in Germany, and an *appetizer* in the US. (Brits are sometimes confused by the US term 'entrée', which implies a start, but is the main course.)

Stilton   strong-tasting blue-veined cheese made in Leicestershire, Nottinghamshire and Derbyshire. Traditionally enjoyed with a glass of port.

swede   large root vegetable; sometimes called 'yellow turnip' or 'rutabaga' in US English

tin   a sealed metal container for food (hence *tinned*: eg 'all we've got for *pudding* is tinned pineapple'); also called a 'can'.

Strangely, in Britain the container seems to be called a *tin* for some foods, but a *can* for other foods – at the supermarket a British shopper might buy a *can of beans* but a *tin of tomatoes*.

tomato sauce   a synonym for tomato ketchup. Can also mean the sauce made from tomatoes that you might enjoy with pasta. Context is everything.

treacle   molasses or dark syrup

trifle   dessert made from a mixture of sponge cake, whipped cream, custard, *jelly*, fruit and sherry or spirits

veg   short for vegetables (eg 'a straightforward meal of meat and two veg'). The term 'veggies' is not used as an abbreviation for 'vegetables', as it is in some other forms of English; a *veggie* in British English is generally a 'vegetarian' (eg 'I've been a veggie since I was 16').

Welsh rarebit   a sophisticated variation of cheese on toast, in which the cheese is seasoned and flavoured with butter, milk and sometimes a little beer. Originally called *Welsh rabbit*. (Maybe a modern Trades Description law forced the name change.)

Worcestershire sauce   a condiment made from anchovies, chillies, garlic and molasses, among other things, introduced to Britain from Bengal during Victorian times. Although the county *Worcestershire* is pronounced 'woostersheer', this sauce is always called just 'wooster'.

SUCK IT AND SEE

In Britain, *sweets* (young children might say *sweeties*) are the equivalent of what Americans call 'candy', and what the Americans call a 'candy bar' is usually called a *bar of chocolate* in Britain. If you want to buy a 'sucker', you'll have to ask for a *lollipop* or a *lolly*. And Australians, note that for the Brits a *lolly* is a sweet on a stick – not any sweet at all.

Shepherd's pie

Traditionally, the main ingredients of shepherd's pie are potatoes and minced lamb or mutton, but often this dish is made with beef instead of lamb (in which case – according to foodie purists – it should be called 'cottage pie'). Here is the recipe for a 'genuine' shepherd's pie that serves four people:

450g (1lb) minced lamb
450g (1lb) potatoes
300ml (about ½ pint) stock
1 onion
cornflour, salt, pepper, butter

Method

Boil the potatoes, mash them, add butter, mash some more, then put to one side. Chop up the onion. Fry the minced lamb in butter, oil or lard. Add the chopped onion. Fry it all together for 5 to 10 minutes. Add the stock, salt and pepper to taste, and some cornflour mixed with water. Stir it all in. Bring to the boil, then simmer for 20 minutes, stirring occasionally while it thickens. Then put the mix of meat and onion in a large casserole dish, and cover with the mashed potato. Do not mix further: the mix of meat and onion should form the bottom layer; the mashed potato should form the top layer of the 'pie'.

Put a lid on the casserole dish, and bake in an oven (pre-heated to 180°C or 350°F) for about half an hour. After about 20 minutes, remove the lid so the top of the potato goes crispy. To make it really special, you can add some grated cheese at this point, so that it melts over the potato. Serve straight from the oven, with green vegetables.

>

<

Toad-in-the-hole

No cruelty to pond-life is involved in this dish – it's a tradition-al meal of meat in batter. The meat is nearly always sausages, although quite why these cylinders of pork or beef are known as 'toads' remains a mystery. The trick for making a good toad-in-the-hole is getting the batter to rise when you bake it in the oven. This recipe (serving four people) tells you how.

450g (1lb) sausages (pork, beef, mixed pork and beef or vegetarian varieties)
100g (4oz) self-raising flour
300ml (about ½ pint) milk
2 eggs
salt, powdered sage, lard or oil

Method
First make the batter mix by sifting the flour, salt and sage together, then breaking in the eggs, and then slowly stirring in the milk, using a whisk to make it very smooth and creamy. If it ain't smooth it won't rise when you bake it in the oven. Keen chefs like to leave the mix to settle for an hour or two, and if you do this you're even more assured of success.

Using a flat-bottomed dish, bake the sausage in the oven (at about 230°C, 450°F) in enough lard or vegetable oil (purists use fresh beef dripping) to cover the bottom of the dish. When the sausages are lightly cooked, pour in the batter mix. At this point, the lard/oil/dripping must be very hot. The batter should sizzle as you pour it in. The quicker this is done, the more successful the dish – it's all to do with the batter and lard/oil/dripping combining at the right temperature. Put the dish back in the oven for about half an hour. Do not open the door. If the air gets in, the batter will not rise. When cooked, serve immediately, with gravy and – you guessed it – green veg.

>

<

Cawl

One of the most popular traditional dishes of Wales, cawl (pronounced 'kowl') is essentially a thick broth. The ingredients vary considerably; historically they depended on what was available – a few basic vegetables when times were hard, thick chunks of meat in days of plenty. This recipe assumes meat – fresh Welsh lamb or mutton, naturally – is available, and is just one variation among many. Vegetarian options obviously omit the meat and use a wider selection of vegetables.

1kg (just over 2lb) diced lamb or mutton
450g (1lb) potatoes
200g (about 1/2 lb) carrots
1 small swede
2 large leeks
flour, chopped parsley, salt, pepper

Method

Cover the meat in water in a big saucepan, and bring to the boil. Dice the carrots and swede, slice the leeks, and add them (with salt and pepper). Simmer the whole lot for about two hours. Cut the potatoes, sprinkle with flour then add to the pan, and simmer for another half an hour. A few minutes before serving, add the chopped parsley. Serve in bowls, and enjoy with thick hunks of crusty bread spread with Welsh butter.

Drinks & drinking

In Britain a *drink* means any ingestible liquid, so if a British person asks if you'd like a drink, don't automatically expect a beer or a whisky. They may well be offering a *cuppa* – a cup of tea – the British national drink.

NON-ALCOHOLIC DRINKS

Following are some terms used to describe non-alcoholic drinks:

cordial   sweetened fruit drink

lemonade   lemon-flavoured carbonated soft drink. Only the term **handmade lemonade** means freshly squeezed lemon juice, water and sugar.

pop   any carbonated soft drink

squash   fruit drink concentrate mixed with water

White or black?   the British way of asking if you'd like milk in your tea or coffee

---

KEEP IT REAL

A nice cup of tea might be the favourite British drink, but a nice pint of beer isn't far behind. For some visitors to Britain, a traditional **bitter** (also known as **real ale**) may come as a warm, flat and expensive shock. This is partly to do with Britain's climate (it's not hot, so beer doesn't need to be cold), and partly with the beer being served by hand-pump rather than gas-pressure.

Most important, though, is the integral flavour: traditional British beer doesn't *need* to be chilled or fizzed. Another key feature of real ale is that it must be stored and served with care (that's why many pubs don't serve it). Beware of places which give the barrels as much care as the condom machine in the toilets. There's nothing worse than a bad pint of real ale – you might as well have a bottle of cheap lager.

ALCOHOLIC DRINKS

A lot of beer and wine in Britain is bought at a supermarket or **off-licence** (a shop selling alcohol to be consumed elsewhere – it might be called a 'liquor store' or 'bottle shop' in other countries). However, large quantities are also consumed at the *pub* – short for 'public house' – the common term for Britain's traditional drinking establishment. (More modern places are called a *bar*, rather than a pub.)

People generally have a favourite pub near their home that they call their *local*. In villages, towns and city suburbs it's a place for neighbours to gather and chat, making the pub effectively an informal meeting room at the heart of the community.

Inner-city pubs can have a different feel from their country or suburban cousins, however. They're often busier, with less of a local feel – but often still a perfect place for a *pint*.

Here are some terms used by British *tipplers*:

ale typical British beer is technically called *ale*, but in practice is more commonly called *bitter*. It's dark brown in colour and generally served at room temperature. *Ale* is also used as a synonym for 'beer', or for 'drinking', whatever alcoholic beverage is consumed (eg 'We're going for a few ales' or 'There was a lot of ale talking last night and some big promises made'). Ale should not be confused with *lager* – see the definition on the page opposite.

bevvy (slang) an alcoholic drink; hence *bevvying* means 'drinking'. The word can also be used to imply an evening of drinking, as in 'Are you coming for a bevvy tonight?'

bitter generally used as a synonym for ale, as opposed to *lager*

BYO on a restaurant sign, an indication that you can *Bring Your Own* alcoholic drinks to a restaurant – usually one that doesn't have a licence to sell these drinks

CHEERS, M'DEARS

Cheers is the usual salutation when raising a glass. But in other circumstances it also means 'thanks' or 'goodbye'. As with so many words in British English, context is everything.

ONE FOR YOURSELF

In British pubs, drinks are ordered and paid for at the bar, and it's not usual to tip the bar staff (unlike in America). However, if you're ordering a large round, or the service has been good all evening, you can say to the person behind the bar *... and one for yourself*. They will add the cost of a drink to your bill – and either keep the money as a tip, or use it to buy a drink later when they're off duty.

cider alcoholic drink made from apples, similar in strength to beer (not a spirit)

corkage the fee charged by restaurants for the *BYO* wines you brought

double in British pubs, spirits are served in measures called *singles* and *doubles*. A *single* is 35ml – just over one US fluid ounce. A *double* is of course 70ml – still disappointingly small when compared to measures in other countries!

free house a pub that doesn't belong to a brewery or pub company, thus is 'free' to sell any brewer's beer. Unfortunately, it doesn't mean the beer is free of charge. The opposite is a *tied house* – see below.

lager a beer that's generally yellow in colour and served cold (eg Foster's or Carling), unlike *ale*

lager top lager with a dash of lemonade. You can also get a *cider top* or a *bitter top*.

local the neighbourhood or village pub. *Going down the local* is a great British pastime.

martini in Britain, this is a small glass of dry vermouth (a wine flavoured with herbs). In the US, a martini is a cocktail made with gin and dry vermouth (a 'dry' martini has the merest dash of vermouth), so Americans in Britain can sometimes feel they're only getting half the drink they ordered.

MINE'S A PINT

A *pint* is the measure in which most beer is sold in Britain. A *British pint*, or an *imperial pint*, as it's still known in these post-colonial days, is just under 20 fluid ounces, or about 570ml. This is larger than a US pint, which is 16 fluid ounces or about 475ml.

But don't worry about the figures, the most important thing it means is 'a drink', as in 'Let's go for a pint after work tonight' – and it might very well mean more than just one.

If you don't want a pint, you can ask for a *half* (a half-pint), but either way, you need to specify the quantity when you're ordering (eg 'Two pints of lager and a packet of crisps please'). Unless you're buying bottled beer, of course …

neat   referring to how a drink is taken, and meaning not mixed with water or a soft drink. Equivalent terms include *straight* (but not 'straight up' in British English – that means 'honestly').

off-licence   a shop licensed to sell alcohol to 'be consumed off the premises', ie to take away. Shortened to *offie* or *beer-off* in some parts of Britain.

Pimms   a popular English spirit, usually served mixed with lemonade, mint, fresh fruit and ice; enjoyed especially in summer

round   several drinks bought at the same time, generally for a group of friends. It's usually reciprocal. If someone says *It's your round*, or *Go and get a round in*, they mean that it's your turn to buy everyone in the group a drink. An impoverished friend might say 'Sorry, guys, I can't get in a round. I've only got a couple of quid on me, so I'll have to buy me own.'

scrumpy a type of strong dry *cider* [from] England's West Country. Many pubs serve it [from the] barrel.

shandy a popular drink in Britain consist[ing] and lemonade mixed together in equal quant[ity] astonishing to some visitors. When ordering, you [should] specify whether you want a *bitter shandy* or a *lager* [shandy].

shout a colloquial term meaning 'to buy a drink or drinks for others'. *My shout* means 'I'll pay'. If someone says *It's your shout*, they mean 'It's your turn to buy'.

snakebite an equal mix of *cider* and *lager*. Favoured by students, as it reputedly gets you drunk quickly and cheaply – thanks to the lager's bubbles and the cider's strength.

snug from a word meaning 'warm', this is usually a small separate room in a pub, or sometimes an enclosed part of a larger room. Traditionally, snugs have a coal fire.

stout a dark, full-bodied beer made from malt. Guinness is the most famous variety.

WATER OF LIFE

The word *whisky* (always spelt without an *e* in Britain, when describing Scotland's most famous export) is derived from the Scottish Gaelic *uisge beatha* – pronounced *oosh·kuh beh·huh* – which literally means 'water of life'.

The two main kinds of whisky are *single malt whisky*, made from malted barley; and *blended whisky*, made from unmalted grain which is then blended with one or more malt whiskies. The quality of blended whisky can vary. Single malts are usually better quality, rarer (there are only about 100 brands) and more expensive.

When ordering a *dram* (a drink of whisky) in Scotland remember to ask for whisky – only the English and other foreigners say 'Scotch'. What else would you be served in Scotland?

Drinks & drinking

__se a pub which is limited to selling the products of a particular brewery, thus making it 'tied' to that brewer. The opposite is a *free house*.

tipple an old-fashioned word for a drink ('Do you fancy a tipple?'). A *tippler* is a drinker.

THAT'S THE SPIRIT

Pubs and bars offer spirits which are often drunk with a mixer, producing British favourites such as *gin and tonic*, *rum and coke* and *vodka and lime*. Only the more up-market city bars in Britain have the vast array of cocktail options you would find in American bars.

If you want to take a shortcut into the heart of British culture, watch the British at play. They're fierce and passionate about their sport, whether participating or watching. The mood of the nation is more closely aligned to the success of its international teams than to budget announcements from the Chancellor of the Exchequer or even the weather forecasts.

Britain gave the world many of its most popular sports, including football, rugby and golf – and then the world started beating the creators at their own games. But that doesn't dampen British enthusiasm. There's always a major sporting event happening somewhere that preoccupies the nation.

Football

Some people may know this game as 'soccer', but in Britain it's definitely called *football*, and it's by far the most popular sport in the country.

SOCK IT TO ME

Football is officially called *association football*, to distinguish it from *rugby football* – the official name for rugby – as well as from Gaelic football, American football, Australian Rules football, and other variations. The word 'soccer' (the favoured term in countries where football means another game) is reputedly an abbreviation of 'Association'; although another theory holds that it's derived from the term 'sock'. In Medieval times a 'sock' was a tough leather foot-covering, worn especially by peasants – just the types who'd enjoy kicking around a pig's bladder with a bunch of mates on a Saturday afternoon.

It's been played for many centuries, although it's unclear exactly when an inter-village competition involving two unruly mobs kicking around a pig's bladder developed into the 'beautiful game'. Scholars put it sometime in the 12th century.

In the following 800 years, and despite repeated royal bans, the game grew in popularity. In the 19th century, the Football Association was founded and the formal rules of the game as we know it today were laid down.

BE A SPORT

Generally speaking, the Brits refer to *sport* in the singular. For example, a fan might say: 'I love sport, me. Football, cricket, horseracing – all of them.'

THE LEAGUES & TEAMS

The English League comprises four *divisions*. At the zenith is the elite *Premier League*, for the country's top 20 clubs – including globally renowned Manchester United, Chelsea, Arsenal and Liverpool. Seventy-two other teams play in the lesser divisions: Championship, League One and League Two (renamed from Divisions 1, 2 and 3 in 2004 – an attempt, say cynics, to make them seem more exciting).

After each season (from August to May) the teams that finish near the bottom of each league get relegated to the next division down, and the teams that finish near the top of the lower division get promoted to the next level up.

Scotland has a separate (though smaller) league structured in the same way as England's. The teams from England and Scotland don't play any domestic games against one another but occasionally meet in European competition. Two teams from Glasgow – Celtic and Rangers – have dominated the Scottish Premier League since its inception in 1874.

In Wales, football is less popular, although some of the bigger teams – Wrexham, Cardiff City and Swansea City – play in the English League.

THE RULES

Disregarding the notorious *offside* rule (which nearly every newcomer to the game has difficulty grasping), football is remarkably straightforward. The aim of each team is to score a *goal* by kicking the round-shaped ball between the posts and under the crossbar of the opposition's *goal*, while at the same time defending their own goal.

Players are allowed to use any part of their body except their hands and arms to block or control the ball, but only the feet and head may be used for striking it.

There are 11 players on each team and five *substitutes* (usually called *subs*) *on the bench* (ie at the side of the pitch) ready to join the game at a moment's notice if another player is injured or called off by the manager. Up to three subs can be used during a game to replace any of the original 11.

Matches have two 45-minute halves with a 15-minute interval in between. Although football is a contact sport, players aren't allowed to grab, tug, strike or kick opponents, or push them with their hands. Firm use of the shoulders when players are running for the ball is allowed, however.

7

Football is a very low-scoring game compared to most team sports – the lack of goals may be one of the reasons football isn't so popular in the US or Australia. No-score draws are reasonably common, but for fans this doesn't mean football isn't entertaining. It's the quality of the play, the tension, the chances and the near misses that make the game – although a goal or two (for the side you support) always puts the icing on the cake.

THE POSITIONS

The players in each team fall into three main types: *attackers* (or *strikers*), *defenders* and *midfielders* (who act as a link between the attackers and defenders and are also often involved in attack and defence themselves). The *goalkeeper* (often shortened to *goalie* or *keeper*) is confined to the goal area. Teams play various formations to get the best result out of each game. A standard formation is *4-4-2*, which means there are four defenders, four midfielders and two strikers. A more attacking formation would be *3-5-2*, where the team decides to play only three defenders and an extra midfielder in order to put more pressure on the opposition's goal.

THE FA CUP

The Football Association held its first interclub knockout tournament in 1871. Fifteen clubs took part, playing for a nice piece of silverware called the FA Cup – then worth about £20. Nowadays, around 600 clubs compete for this legendary and priceless trophy. It differs from many other competitions in that every team – from the lowest-ranking part-timers to the stars of the Premier League – is in with a chance. The team with the most FA Cup victories is Manchester United (a total of ten), but public attention is invariably focused on the 'giant-killers' – minor clubs that claw their way up through the rounds, unexpectedly beating higher-ranking competitors. One of the best-known giant-killing events occurred in 1992, when Wrexham, then ranked 24th in Division 3, famously beat league champions Arsenal.

THE HIGHLIGHTS

Each football season kicks off with the *Charity Shield* – a match between the winners of the previous year's Premier League and FA Cup competitions. The season climaxes in May each year with the *FA Cup Final* – traditionally held at Wembley Stadium in North London, but with a few years out at Cardiff's Millennium Stadium while Wembley was being rebuilt.

Some British football terms you might hear include:

booking   a warning to a player from the referee, usually after committing a *foul* (breaking a rule of the game). 'Jones deliberately kicked Smith. It was a clear foul and Jones got a booking for it.' Or '... and Jones was booked for it.'

cross   this means kicking the ball across the pitch, instead of up or down. It's often used when the ball is kicked across the face of the goal in an attempt to score.

half-time   the break halfway through the game

header   when a player strikes the ball with the head, rather than the foot

kick-off   the start of the game

offside   an attacking player can't be passed the ball by another player on the same team if there's no player from the opposing team between them and the goal. If this happens the attacking player receiving the ball is offside. A strategy often employed by defending players is to move forward (ie away from their goal) so that a player from the attacking side suddenly finds themselves in an *offside position*, and unable to receive the ball. The rule was developed to prevent *goal-hanging* (waiting very close to the goal).

penalty   a free shot at the goal awarded when a defending player fouls an attacking opponent in the area in front of the goal (called the *penalty box*). Penalties are taken from the *penalty spot*.

red card a player committing a serious foul is ***booked*** (see above) then shown a ***yellow card*** by the referee. A player getting two yellow cards in the same game is then shown a ***red card*** and expelled from the game. If the foul is serious enough, the player may be shown the red card without an initial warning.

referee's assistant proper name for an official who monitors the game from the side of the pitch – there are two at most matches. The common name for this official is a ***linesman***. At some matches there's also a ***fourth official*** – acting as an extra pair of eyes to help the referee and the assistant referees.

skipper a colloquial term for the team captain, who normally wears an armband to indicate captaincy

sweeper a defensive position – a player who 'sweeps away' the ball if it's passed towards the goal

yellow card see ***red card***

SPORTING GENTLEMEN

A wit once said that football is a gentlemen's game played by hooligans, while rugby is the other way around – a hooligan's game played by gentlemen. (Irish or Gaelic football, incidentally, is said to be a hooligan's game played by hooligans.)

Cricket

The quintessentially English game of cricket (it's far more popular in England than in Wales or Scotland) has been played formally since the 18th century – although its roots go much further back. Cricket became an international game during Britain's colonial era, when it was exported to the countries of the Commonwealth, particularly the Indian subcontinent, the West Indies and Australasia.

If you're unfamiliar with the game, you may see cricket as a form of torture. It's so slow. Nothing seems to happen for hours. Surely, this is the game for which TV highlights were invented! However, if you're patient and learn the intricacies, you could find cricket as enriching and enticing as all the Brits do who remain glued to their radio or TV all summer, 'just to see how England's getting on'.

THE RULES

A cricket team comprises 11 players. For each *innings* (a team's chance at batting), one team *bats* and the opposing team *bowls*. The bowling team has all its players on the field: one *bowler* and 10 *fielders*. The batting team is represented by two *batsmen* on the *pitch*. The other nine players sit in the *pavilion* waiting for their turn.

The two batsmen each stand in front of a set of *wickets* (three wooden uprights called *stumps*, across which are balanced two smaller wooden cylinders called *bails*) spaced 22 yards apart on the *pitch* (a rectangle of very short grass in the middle of the circular or oval field). The bowler's aim is to get the batsman *out*. The batting team's aim is to score *runs* (points) by hitting the ball as far as possible and running up and down between the wickets. If the batsman does hit the ball, it's the aim of the fielders to catch it before it hits the ground.

The bowler must *bowl* the ball with a straight arm (if the arm is bent it's a *throw*, and against the rules), and is allowed six attempts (called an *over*). The batsmen don't have to attempt to hit each ball bowled to them. Neither do they have to run each time a ball is struck. After these six attempts, the *over* is over (are you keeping up?), and another bowler has another six attempts, bowling at the wicket at the opposite end of the pitch.

The bowler tries to get the batsman *out* or *dismissed* in two main ways: either by hitting the wicket with the ball or by forcing the batsman to strike the ball into the air so that a fielder can catch it before it hits the ground. A third way a batsman can be ruled *out* is if the ball would have hit the wicket, but the batman's body blocks it. In this case the umpire can rule *leg before wicket* (usually shortened to *lbw*).

Also, if the batsmen are running and one of the fielders hits the wickets with the ball and dislodges a bail, then the nearest batsman is *run out* (often simply called *out*), giving rise to cries from the other players of *Howzat!* ('How was that?') to the umpire – this is known as *appealing*. (In total, there are ten ways a batsman can get out, six of which happen fairly regularly, but these are the four main ones.)

When one batsman is out, he's replaced by a new one. The *innings* is over when 10 of the 11 in the team are out.

If the batsman strikes the ball and it reaches the *boundary* (the perimeter of the field of play), he's awarded four runs without the bother of actually having to do any running. If the ball goes over the boundary without bouncing first, he's awarded six runs.

THE COMPETITIONS

The teams that make up the main domestic competition are drawn from counties, including Yorkshire, Warwickshire, Hampshire, and this level of competition is known as *County Cricket*.

The English national cricket team is known as the *MCC*, from Marylebone Cricket Club, and the home of English cricket (indeed of world cricket, many would say) is *Lord's Cricket Ground* in London.

BALLS?

Britain's major ball-sports – football, cricket, rugby league and rugby union – are predominantly played by men, as indicated by terms such as 'batsman' (and the use of 'he' and 'him' throughout this Sport section). However, all these games are played by women too – with the women's national football and cricket teams often enjoying greater (though less publicised) success on the international field than their male counterparts.

International cricket matches are called *tests*. The English team tours each year and hosts at least one tour from one of the other major cricket-playing nations (Australia, India, Pakistan, Sri Lanka, South Africa and the West Indies). The most important of these for English cricket fans is the game against Australia, known as *the Ashes* (see the box below).

In test matches, each team gets two innings and the game can last for five days. Even then, these matches often end in a draw because neither team has time to force a win. If this is your experience after watching your first five-day test you'll (a) be unlucky and (b) probably never want to watch cricket again.

ASHES TO ASHES

The result of a test match between England and Australia is referred to as winning or losing *the Ashes*. This name derives from a mock obituary for English cricket printed in *The Times* newspaper in 1882, following an Australian victory. Until this year, England had dominated the international game. The obituary said that the 'body' (ie of English cricket) was cremated and the ashes taken to Australia. The name stuck, and England and Australia play against one other every two years, alternately in each country, both sides grimly determined to retain, or win, the Ashes.

Rugby union

There are two codes of rugby played in Britain – rugby union and rugby league. *Rugby union* in England is traditionally the game of the middle and upper classes, and at Britain's top schools it is sometimes known as *rugger*.

Rugby union is played more in southern England, Wales and Scotland, while *rugby league* is traditionally played and supported by the working classes, and is played predominantly in northern England – although there's a lot of crossover.

Rugby traces its roots to a football match in 1823 at Rugby School, in Warwickshire, a county in central England. A player called William Ellis, frustrated at the limitations of mere kicking, reputedly picked up the ball and ran with it towards the opponents' goal. True to the sense of British fair play, rather than Ellis being dismissed from the game, a whole new sport was developed around his tactic. The Rugby Football Union (*RFU*) was formally inaugurated nearly 50 years later, in 1871.

THE RULES

There are 15 players in each rugby union team. The aim is to carry the oval-shaped ball across the opponents' goal line and touch the ground. The player's hand must be on the ball as it's pressed down. This is called a *try* and is worth five points. After each try, the scoring team is awarded an opportunity to kick at the H-shaped goal posts. If the ball is successfully kicked between the posts and above the crossbar, a *goal* (also called a *conversion*) is scored and the team is awarded two points. When a goal is scored at any other time in the match by a player kicking the ball, either during play (called a *drop goal* or *field goal*) or when play has been halted because the other side committed an offence (called a *penalty*), it's worth three points.

Rugby is definitely a contact sport: *tackling* (grabbing or stalling) an opposing player is only prohibited above the shoulders – anywhere else on the body is allowed.

The players move the ball forward by carrying it, either running alone or in a *ruck* (see the definition on the page opposite). The ball can also be thrown by hand from one player to another, but not forwards. When a player either deliberately or inadvertently moves the ball forward with his hands, it's called a *knock-on*, and a free ball is awarded to the other team.

The ball may be kicked forward from one player to another, as long as the receiving player was behind the kicking player when the ball was kicked – this is called *running onto the ball*).

THE HIGHLIGHTS

The most important annual competition for Britain's rugby union fans is the *Six Nations Championship*, held from February to March and contested by England, Scotland, Wales, Italy, France and Ireland. (Ireland's team represents both the Republic and Northern Ireland.) Each team plays alternate home and away matches, and plays each of the other teams only once during the competition.

England's home ground is Twickenham (known fondly as *Twickers*) in London. Scotland plays at Murrayfield in Edinburgh, and Wales plays at the Millennium Stadium in Cardiff, on the site of the fabled Cardiff Arms Park.

Within the Six Nations Championship are unofficial awards: if one team from the British Isles (England, Scotland, Wales and Ireland) beats all the others it wins the *Triple Crown*. If any team in the tournament beats all the others, it gets the *Grand Slam*. The last-placed team gets the dreaded *Wooden Spoon*. Some rugby terms include:

ruck   when one or more players from each team are on their feet and in physical contact, supporting a player who's holding the ball, it's called a *ruck* (which in Britain is also a general slang term for a fight). The players help each other push against their opponents in an attempt to gain ground.

scrum   originally a scrum was a disorderly struggle in which each team tried to force the ball and opposing players towards the opposing goal. Today it's an aspect of the game used to accomplish the same thing, but it only happens following an infringement or a breakdown in play. In rugby union, a scrum involves eight players from each side. The *forwards* from each team lock arms and put their heads down. The middle player in each front row is called the *hooker* and the players on either side of him are the *props*. The one at the back is called the *Number 8*. The *scrum half* puts the ball into the heart of the scrum when he thinks his team has the momentum and then races around behind his team-mates to gather the ball when they back-heel it out of the scrum, so that play can continue. That's the theory. In reality it often ends in a great pile-up.

THE OXFORD & CAMBRIDGE BOAT RACE

This famous rowing race between teams of eight from the two oldest universities in England takes place annually in late March or early April. The race dates from 1829 and is billed as the world's longest surviving sporting rivalry. The race distance is 6800m – three times the Olympic distance – and has never been cancelled due to bad weather, despite treacherous conditions which have caused boats to sink in the past.

Rugby league

Rugby league broke away from rugby union in England in the 1890s, when many of the rules changed and it rapidly became professional or semi-professional at the top level. (Rugby union remained ostensibly amateur until the 1990s.)

THE RULES

Many of the rules and tactics in rugby league are similar to those in rugby union, although a major difference is that there are only 13 players in each team. A game consists of two 40-minute halves, with a 10-minute interval.

Players attempt to get the oval ball past their opponents by hand-passing (always backwards) or kicking (usually forwards, but the receiver must have run from behind the kicker).

If an attacking player carrying the ball is tackled and brought to the ground by the opposition, play pauses but (unlike in rugby union) the ball is retained by the attacking side. The defending team moves back, the tackled player regains his feet, heels the ball backwards to a team-mate, and the attack recommences. After six tackles, the other team gets possession of the ball, and their opportunity to score.

Grounding the ball beyond the opponent's goal line is called a *try*, which is worth four points. A try can be *converted*

SPORT

100

into a *goal* by kicking the ball over the crossbar and between the posts of the H-shaped goal (in the same way as in rugby union), for two points. Teams can also score a goal by kicking the ball during play (called a *drop goal*) for one point. A *penalty* goal is worth two points.

Other sports, games & hobbies

BOWLS
Officially known as *lawn bowls*, this is a very old game with a reputation (undeserved) for attracting very old players. It's played with balls called *woods* that have one side weighted (the *bias*) so they run in a curved course. The game is traditionally played outdoors on a *green* (meaning a finely mown grass lawn – sometimes slightly domed, in which case the game is called *crown green bowling*), but there are also indoor tournaments. The players roll their woods at a smaller white ball (the *jack*), trying to get as close to it as possible. And that's it. Sounds simple but it's not. Perhaps only those mature in years have the patience to master the game.

> ## CONKERS
>
> *Conkers* is the name of a game played by children using horse chestnuts, which has been around for at least 400 years. The name may derive from the word 'conquer'. The nuts themselves are also called *conkers*.
>
> What's involved? It's simple. The green shell is peeled off the horse chestnut, and the nut threaded onto a string, knotted at one end to keep the nut from flying off. Each player takes turns swinging their conker at the other person's conker until one of the conkers shatters. That's it. Game over.
>
> If you have a conker that's beaten five others it's called a *fiver*. Likewise, *three-er*, *sixer*, *twelver*, *27-er* and so on – although the *27-er* may well have been lightly baked in the oven before coming into play (a common ploy among the more ambitious inhabitants of the playground).

DON THE ANORAK

An *anorak* is a warm coat or jacket, favoured by *train spotters* and bird-watchers, and thus now a byword for anything or anyone who's a bit obsessive (eg 'Donald spends all day tinkering with his cactus collection – he's a bit of an anorak.')

Incidentally, *anorak* is one of very few words of Inuit (the language of the people commonly known as 'Eskimoes') to be borrowed by English. *Kayak* is another.

DARTS

Darts is primarily a pub game, popular throughout Britain, and many people play in local pub or club teams. But major competitions attract a huge following, and to replicate the atmosphere entire indoor arenas are turned into bars.

The rules are simple: players throw three darts consecutively at a circular board, which is divided up into sections with different numerical values from 1 to 20, plus a small circle in the middle of the dart board called the *bullseye* – worth 50 points. Each section is subdivided, with a small *double* area (so a player hitting the double 20 will score 40 points) and an even smaller *treble* area. Skilled players aim consistently for the treble 20, and if they strike it with all three darts they score 180. At the big games, this results in a drawn-out 'Oner-huuunderrred-and-eighteeee!' shout from the compere, much cheering from the audience, and vast amounts of alcohol being quaffed in celebration.

A player starts with 501 points, and the player's score is deducted from this until he or she reaches zero. Players must finish by hitting a *double* – for example, if there's 36 left to score, they must aim for double 18.

SKITTLES

Skittles is a traditional pub game (played inside or out) in which players roll wooden balls at nine roughly-cylindrical wooden blocks arranged in a diamond pattern. It's also called *ninepins*, and is similar in principle to the game called tenpin bowling. Until the 1980s many pubs had a *skittle alley*, but these days most have fallen into disuse and been turned into extra drinking areas.

There's also a more compact version of this game, called *table skittles*, where the ball is swung on a string.

SNOOKER

Snooker is a game related to pool, but requiring far more skill (say its proponents), and involving a table about four times the size of a pool table. Players use *cues* to strike balls, aiming to *pot* them (get them in pockets). There are 15 red balls and six balls of other colours – yellow, green, brown, blue, pink and black. Each time a red ball is potted, one point is scored and the player gets the opportunity to *pot a colour*. The coloured balls are worth more: two points for the least, yellow, ascending to seven points for the black. The red stays in the pocket after it's potted, but the colours are replaced in their original positions. Once all the reds are potted, the colours must be potted in the order given above.

TRAIN SPOTTING

As the name suggests, *train spotting* is the hobby of looking out for trains and collecting their numbers. It's surprisingly popular. No major rail station is complete without groups of *train spotters* – men and boys (very few women) armed with notebooks at vantage points such as the platform-ends, watching the trains come in and out.

OTHER SPORTING TERMS

Other British terms to do with sport or games include:

bird-watching a very popular British hobby – the observation of wild birds. Also called *birding*, and a bird-watcher might be called a *birder*. Some bird-watchers like to see as many different species as they can (see the *twitcher* definition following), but most are happy just to observe bird behaviour even if they've

THE CUTTING EDGE OF TRAIN SPOTTING

Train spotter has become a deprecatory term for a boring or obsessive person. *Train spotting* is also slang for heroin use, supposedly because addicts are obsessed with scoring the next hit or finding a clean vein to inject into, although it's not a term favoured by drug users themselves. The 1990s film *Trainspotting* – about heroin users in Edinburgh – brought the term into mainstream parlance. (The slang term *track*, meaning a line of needle marks or an infected vein, is another train-related link.)

In the world of clubs and dance music, *train spotters* are the music fans who loiter around the DJ's mixing desk to see what music's being played or how one track (yes, another train link) is blended into another.

seen certain species many times before – although spotting a species for the first time is always exciting.

draughts   (pronounced 'drafts'); called 'checkers' in the US

lawn tennis   lawn tennis is the proper name for the game usually known simply as 'tennis'. It's called lawn tennis because it was originally played on a grass court, and to distinguish it from 'real tennis' (an older form of the sport played inside a court and bouncing the ball off the walls as well as the floor). It's correctly called lawn tennis today, even when it's played on clay or concrete courts.

noughts and crosses   game played with a pen and paper; called 'tick-tack-toe' in the US

pitch   the field of play – hence football pitch, cricket pitch, and so on

sledge   used for sliding on snow; called a 'sled' in the US

twitcher   an obsessive bird-watcher, one who often goes to great lengths to see as many bird species as possible. Note that the term does not apply to all bird-watchers or amateur ornithologists, only to the obsessive ones. Nothing annoys a ***birder*** more than being called a ***twitcher*** (unless they are one).

ENTERTAINMENT

Since the dawn of the swinging '60s, Britain has been firmly on the main stage of pop and rock music. There's a thriving cinema industry too, although it's often overshadowed by Hollywood. And British theatre continues to live up to its reputation as the finest in the world; London's West End is *the* international centre for performing arts – whatever New Yorkers say!

Theatre & cinema

CINEMA
The British cinema industry has its *ups and downs* (high points and low points), but the directors never fail to produce a wide range of films that are witty, challenging or just downright good. A common characteristic of British films is their reliance on dialogue or characterisation rather than, for example, computer-generated imagery and endless special effects – one happy outcome of low budgets and tough conditions.

Note that Brits talk more about *films* than *movies*, even though the latter term is sometimes favoured by aficionados. Likewise, the US term 'movie theatre' is rarely used; Brits go to the *cinema*.

Some other cinema-related terms include:

concession   this means a discount. *Concession tickets* are cheaper tickets available at the cinema or theatre for senior citizens, students and so on.

flicks   an old-fashioned term for the cinema ('Are you going to the flicks with us tonight?'), so called because the images used to flicker on the screen. Hence *Brit-flick* – a British-made film.

pictures   another old-fashioned term for the cinema ('Are you going to the pictures with us tonight?')

Theatre & cinema

105

trailer a preview (of an upcoming film) shown before the main film. Yep, the trailers come first.

THEATRE

The shows of the *West End* (central London's theatre district; Britain's version of America's Broadway) are the best known, but great drama, comedy and musicals can be seen at theatres in towns and cities across the country. Theatre-related terms in Britain include:

gods the upper balconies of a theatre, so called because they're so high up you're near heaven. Seats here are usually the cheapest, and the last to be sold because the view of the stage can be poor.

pantomime a light-hearted theatrical performance, in which a fairy tale or nursery story (*Cinderella*, *Little Red Riding Hood*, *Babes in the Wood*, etc) is dramatised – usually with music and dancing, frequent ad-libbing and numerous contemporary references. *Pantomimes* are a favourite form of family entertainment during the Christmas and New Year season. And despite the name, they are not done in mime.

stalls seats on the floor of a theatre, as opposed to in the balcony

ALL AROUND THE GLOBE

The famous Globe Theatre on London's South Bank is forever associated with Britain's best-known playwright, William Shakespeare. The original Globe Playhouse was built in 1598–99 and closed in 1642, just 26 years after Shakespeare's death.

In 1997, a replica Globe Theatre opened very close to the original location. It was constructed to reflect the original as closely as possible, and so performances take place under the open sky, with seating *in the round* (circling the stage) on wooden benches for an audience of 1000 and standing room for 500 *groundlings*.

Radio & TV

TV and radio broadcasting in Britain is dominated by the **British Broadcasting Corporation** (**BBC**), a venerable and much-loved national public service institution. Foreigners are often amazed that the BBC can produce such a range of professional, innovative and stimulating programmes – and all without advertisements!

In national radio broadcasting there's:

- Music station BBC Radio 1 (aimed at a predominantly young audience)
- BBC Radio 2 (for the folks who got too old for Radio 1)
- BBC Radio 3 (predominantly classical, but covers jazz and world music too)
- BBC Radio 4 (news, comment, analysis, current affairs, drama and humour)
- BBC Radio 5 Live (sport and talk – often dubbed *Radio Bloke*).

Across the borders from England, the locals tune into BBC Radio Scotland and BBC Radio Wales.

Turning to TV, Britain has five **terrestrial** channels (ie free-to-air, as opposed to cable and satellite):

- BBC1 and BBC2 are publicly funded and don't carry advertising.
- ITV, Channel 4 and Channel 5 are commercial stations.

Additionally, Scottish Television (STV) carries Gaelic-speaking programmes and Wales has *S4C* or *Siannel 4 Cymru* (Channel 4 Wales).

DON'T BOOB

The American term 'boob tube' is not used in Britain to mean 'television'. In Britain, *boobs* is slang for breasts, and a *boob tube* is a tight-fitting strapless top. *Boob* also means mistake, which is what you'd be making if you used this term in the wrong context.

Britain is currently switching from analogue to digital broadcasting; as part of the process, new free-to-air digital channels – such as BBC3, BBC4, ITV3 and 4 More – are also available.

Some other terms relating to broadcasting include:

Auntie   term of endearment for the BBC

Beeb   another term of endearment for the BBC

chat show   a TV show based around entertaining interviews, rather than, say, news or music

dumbed down   an accusation frequently levelled at TV producers on free-to-air channels, meaning that they've dropped the quality of their programmes in order to chase ratings, in the face of competition from cable and satellite stations

programme   what the Americans call a TV or radio 'show', the Brits generally call a *programme*

tabloid television   TV programmes that ape the style and tone of popular (or 'tabloid') newspapers – short on analysis, hot on gossip

watershed   the time in the evening after which there are fewer restrictions on TV content. It's currently 9pm or 9.30pm – on the assumption that children are safely tucked up in bed and won't be exposed to post-watershed swearing, violence and nudity.

Music & clubs

Britain has long been a major player in pop and rock music. Although America led the way in the years after World War II, by the 1960s Britain was getting in on the act, with early exports including the Beatles, the Rolling Stones, the Who, the Kinks and Welsh soul-man Tom Jones.

By the 1970s, a notable genre of British music was *glam rock*, exemplified by stardust-speckled heroes like Marc Bolan and David Bowie. *Prog rock* (progressive rock) was another genre of the time, incorporating features of jazz and classical music. By the early '80s, however, prog rock heroes such as Genesis, Pink Floyd and Led Zeppelin were considered outdated, self-indulgent *dinosaur bands*. The new sound was *punk music* – energetic, anarchic and with a DIY approach ('Here's three chords, now form a band' ran a famous quote in a *fanzine*) – and it returned pop to the grassroots, at least for a while. Notable British punk bands included the Sex Pistols

(famous for one album and a clutch of mostly banned singles), the Clash, the Damned and the Buzzcocks.

Then punk begat another genre: *new wave* (ie everything that was a bit punky), with leading exponents including the Jam, the Tourists and Elvis Costello.

Around this time, another British speciality – *heavy metal* – enjoyed an upsurge, with bands such as Black Sabbath (featuring Ozzy Osbourne) and Judas Priest exporting soulful melodies and intriguing interpretations of established religion to concert halls worldwide.

The 1980s also saw a surge of *electronica* being produced by the likes of Depeche Mode, Cabaret Voltaire and Human League. It overlapped with the *New Romantic* scene, which featured bands such as Spandau Ballet, Duran Duran and Culture Club – all frills and fringes, and a definite swing of pop's pendulum away from the untidy punks.

In 1983 in the musical hotbed of Manchester, arguably Britain's second city, a band called New Order (formed from the ashes of Joy Division) released the seminal track *Blue Monday*, combining the guitar sound of punk with a pulsating beat of a new sound called *dance*. This fed into the development of the British *rave* scene, with music influenced by the US *house* genre, often played at massive illegal parties in fields or derelict industrial sites. The raves in turn popularised the drug ecstasy and launched the careers of many top DJs, as well as starting the evolution of just about every *dance music* genre.

The heady mix of dance and rock music peaked in the late-80s to early-90s, still centred on Manchester and epitomised by bands like the Stone Roses and the Happy Mondays. It became known simply as the *Manchester sound*, and thanks to the abundance of innovation and good times, the city itself was dubbed *Madchester.*

Building on the success of the Manchester sound, the '90s also saw the renaissance of *indie* bands – *indie* (from 'independent') implying a type of music, or approach to music, favoured by smaller independent record labels, as opposed to the more commercial sound favoured by big labels. The likes of Blur, Supergrass, Ocean Colour Scene, Manic Street Preachers, the Verve, Pulp, Travis, Feeder, Super

Furry Animals, Stereophonics, Catatonia and, above all, Oasis revived the flagging guitar-based format. Heralded as the *Britpop* revolution, it's largely thanks to these bands that the *indie* guitar sound remained such a major feature of British pop music when it entered the 21st century.

Other British musical genres of the late 1990s and early 2000s include:

breaks also known as *breakbeat* or *nu skool breakbeat*. A lively 'bouncy' upfront style, halfway between *house* and *drum and bass*.

bhangra this is the name for a style of traditional music from the Punjab region of South Asia; in recent times it's also become the term for a style of music invented in Britain (though now exported around the world), which mixes traditional Punjabi styles with modern pop, rap, dance and reggae music – among others

drum and bass dance music emphasising fast, heavy beats and strong bass; also known as *jungle*. Originally a British genre, though it spread quickly. Influences on drum and bass include *oldskool* rave, house, techno, hip-hop and even ragga (a type of electronic reggae).

grime a very hardcore mix of *garage* and *drum and bass*. Usually has fast rough beats and often very explicit or provocative vocals.

THE PROMS

The best known of all British classical music concert programmes is **the Proms** (short for 'promenade concerts' because people used to walk about, or stand, while they listened). It's one of the world's greatest music festivals. Concerts are held from mid-July to mid-September each year at the Royal Albert Hall in London, and are widely broadcast on TV and radio.

The US term 'prom' is not used in Britain – **the Proms** have nothing to do with high-school dances.

trip-hop   a musical style derived from hip-hop but slower in tempo, pioneered most notably by bands and artists from the city of Bristol, such as Massive Attack, Portishead and Tricky. Also known as the *Bristol sound*.

UK garage   also known as *2 step*. Whereas the US *garage* sound is nearer house music and has an emphasis on vocal melodies, the UK version includes more influences from hip-hop and urban street culture.

The coverage above of dance music genres brings us inevitably to the world of clubs. In Britain, London is indisputably the number one spot for *clubbing*, but the cities of Brighton, Bristol, Cardiff, Nottingham, Glasgow, Manchester, Sheffield, Swansea, Edinburgh, Leeds and Liverpool all have large and thriving club scenes as well, where top DJs and wild theme nights bring in eager *clubbers* to enjoy *tracks*, *tunes* and *cuts* – a lot of them on *vinyl* ('old-fashioned' records as opposed to CDs or other digital media).

In British club terminology, *club* doesn't necessarily refer to a place. (The place is also called a *venue*.) A *club* can be an entity encapsulating the regular DJs and *punters* (customers), the type of music, the overriding theme and the general vibe. This is also called a *club night*, simply a *night*, or a *session* (eg 'a breaks night' or 'the regular Gatecrasher night at the Ministry of Sound'). Just to keep you on your toes, some club names and venue names are synonymous. Others aren't.

A small selection of live music and club terms you may hear include:

air guitar   when rock fans mime a guitar-playing motion, usually in time with the live band's performance, they're *playing the air guitar*

B-boy   originally a US term for a breakdancer; in the UK context it can refer to any hip-hop fan who looks the part

bouncer   door steward at a club or venue (even some pubs), usually with the power to decide who can enter and who can't. The term can also mean a security steward within a club or concert employed to eject miscreants.

A BIT OF A SONG & DANCE

The Gaelic word *ceilidh* (pronounced 'kaylee'), meaning 'visit', originally referred to a social gathering in the home in Scotland. There'd be music and singing, and a local bard to relate poems, stories and legends. These days, a *ceilidh* means an organised evening of *folk* (traditional) entertainment, including music, singing and dance.

Choooon! (translation: 'tune') cry of appreciation from clubbers meaning 'that's a great track!'

E ecstasy, a recreational drug favoured by clubbers

headbang heavy metal fans used to show appreciation of their favourite genre by shaking their heads forward and back in time to the music – sometimes with a violence that caused brain damage. Today a *head-banger* can be any crazy person or concept. For example: 'That Gary's a bit of a head-banger, always looking for fights in pubs' or 'To adopt more pro-European policies is a head-banging idea.'

heavy a term with numerous uses, from simply 'loud and hard' (eg 'heavy bass', 'heavy metal') to 'very cool' (for example: 'That mix is heavy')

large in the context of clubbing or entertainment generally, *having a large one* (or simply *having it large*) is having a big night out. Hence also *larging it*.

mosh pit the area in front of the stage at a live performance, where the fans dance most enthusiastically

phat cool; heavy

pills in the context of clubbing, *pills* usually means ecstasy. For example, the friendly stranger in the toilets may ask 'Need any pills?'

mash-up a club mix putting together various styles of music

pogo a form of enthusiastic dancing which involves jumping up and down vertically in time to the music. ***Pogoing*** was pioneered by punks but is now enjoyed by fans of other genres. The style supposedly developed at crowded concerts where there was no room to do anything else.

punters this word originally meant the people attending a horse-race (***to punt*** means 'to bet'), but now refers to people at any event such as a rock concert or a club (eg 'On Gatecrasher's big nights there's always a long queue of punters trying to get in')

residency a DJ's regular (usually weekly or monthly) slot at a particular club

Festivals

Britain hosts a plethora of festivals, most – but not all – held in the summer when the weather is likely to be better. The list below (in alphabetical order) outlines a selection of the main events:

Bath International Music Festival top-class classical music and opera, plus jazz and world music (mid-May to early June, Bath)

Braemar Gathering with over 20,000 people, including the Royals, 'gathering' is an understatement for this famous Highland knees-up (first Saturday of September, Braemar, Deeside, in Scotland)

Chelsea Flower Show blooming marvellous floral feast (late May, London)

Edinburgh Fringe held concurrently with the Edinburgh International Festival, ***the Fringe*** offers hundreds of amateur and professional offbeat and avant-garde performances (August, Edinburgh)

Edinburgh International Festival   one of the world's largest and most important arts festivals, overshadowed only by its own Fringe festival (August, Edinburgh)

Edinburgh Military Tattoo   three weeks of pageantry and soldierly displays (August, Edinburgh)

Euro Pride   Europe's largest gay and lesbian march and festival (late June to early July, London)

Glastonbury Festival   huge open-air happening with hippy roots, involving three days of music, dance, camping – and, frequently, mud (late June, Somerset)

Glyndebourne Opera Festival   world-class opera in a country-house garden (late-May to August, Lewes, Sussex)

Guy Fawkes Night   firework and bonfire celebrations held to commemorate the failure, in the year 1605, of an attempt to assassinate the king and Parliament (5 November, nationwide)

International Eisteddfod   music festival bringing together a lively mix of cultures from Wales and far beyond (July, Llangollen)

Jorvik Viking Festival   horned helmets galore, plus mock invaders and Viking longship races (February, York)

HIGHLAND GAMES

Held throughout the summer at towns and villages across Scotland, *highland games* involve music and dancing competitions and sporting events, such as *tossing the caber* (heaving a tree trunk as far as possible) and *throwing the hammer*. Originally, the games were organised by clan chiefs who'd recruit the strongest competitors for their army or bodyguard. Today, the winners just get the glory.

Notting Hill Carnival   a spectacular Caribbean-style multi-cultural feast (late August, London)

Reading Festival   three-day open-air rock, pop and dance extravaganza (late August, Reading, Berkshire)

Royal Highland Show   Scotland's national display-piece with big-horned cattle, cabers, bagpipes, kilts – the lot (late June, Edinburgh)

Royal Welsh Show   national agricultural and cultural gathering (mid-July, Builth Wells)

Sesiwn Fawr   three-day rock, folk and beer bash in the heart of Wales (July, Dollgellau)

T in the Park   open-air pop, rock and dance music festival – Scotland's answer to Glastonbury (July, Glasgow)

Womad   global gathering of world and roots music (late July, Reading, Berkshire)

Shopping

In addition to music, cinema and theatre, shopping is a major entertainment or leisure activity in Britain, as in many countries. It's about so much more than simply buying necessities – although some people would say that a new tie, a new handbag or just one more pair of those nice-looking shoes in the window *is* an absolute necessity.

Here are some terms that are frequently used in the boutiques, supermarkets and high streets of Britain:

advert   an abbreviation for ***advertisement***, be it on TV, in a shop window or on a large ***hoarding***. (The latter item is called a 'billboard' in the US.)

bob   a colloquial term for ***shilling***, a unit of currency discontinued in Britain in the early 1970s. (A pound contained

20 shillings.) More than 30 years later the term is still used occasionally: so £2.50 in modern currency might be called *fifty bob* and the modern 50p piece a *ten-bob bit*. You might also hear someone say: 'Look, it's not expensive, it's only a couple of bob.'

building society a financial institution primarily focused on providing loans for home-buyers, and usually *mutual* (ie owned by members, not shareholders). They are known as 'savings and loan banks' in the US. Building societies are not banks (a major difference is that they're not owned by shareholders), but they offer many similar services. Many British building societies have 'demutualised' to become banks in recent decades.

car-boot sale a public sale of old or unused household items, similar in principle to the 'garage sales' or sales that people hold in their driveways in other countries. However, the *car-boot sale* generally takes place in a car park or field on the edge of town, with everyone bringing the stuff they want to sell in the *boot* (that's 'trunk' to Americans) of their car. The original idea was to sell items out of the boot of the car, but these days people spread them out on the ground or a table.

NOT WORTH TUPPENCE HA'PENNY

In Britain's pre-decimal currency system, a *pound* contained 20 shillings and a *shilling* contained 12 pennies: so a pound contained 240 pennies. In colloquial speech, *pennies* were called *pence* – five pennies was called *fivepence*, three pennies was *thruppence* and two pennies was *tuppence*. The price 'two pounds, three shillings and sixpence' might be written £2-3-6, while three shillings and sixpence (shortened to *three and six*) might be written 3/6. There were also *half-pennies* (always called *ha'pennies*) and *farthings* (quarters of a penny). Imagine the fun pre-1970s school kids had simply learning to add up their pocket money!

OLD JOKES' HOME

Bill loans £6 to Ben. The next day Ben gives Bill an ill-looking octopus. Bill says, 'What's this?' Ben replies, 'It's that sick squid I owe you.' Say it out loud. Don't you just love wordplay?

chemist a shop selling prescription and non-prescription medicines. Many other countries use the term 'pharmacy' (which is also used in Britain) or 'drug store'. As well as medicines, at most chemists you can usually buy perfume, cosmetics, soap and *toiletries* (stuff you might use in the bathroom). Larger *high street* chemists sell an even broader range of goods, including ready-to-eat food and photographic supplies.

custom a synonym for 'business' or 'patronage'. In Britain you hear phrases like, 'They get a lot of custom in that shop' or 'I won't give him my custom any more.'

fiver a colloquial term for a five-pound note. (Brits also use the term *tenner*, but not 'twentier'.)

greengrocer a shop selling fruit and vegetables; also a person working in the shop

high street primary street or road in a town where the bulk of the shops are – the butcher, the baker, the greengrocer, the newsagent, the chemist and so on

ironmongery hardware store

Marks & Sparks nickname for one of the most popular department stores in Britain, *Marks & Spencer*

p (pronounced 'pee') the abbreviation for *pennies* or *pence*, and often used in everyday speech. So 50p is pronounced 'fifty pee'.

pound the main unit of currency in Britain, also called the *sterling pound* or *pound sterling*. There are 100 pennies in a pound. The pound symbol (£) is derived from the letter *L*, as the Latin for 'pound' is *libre*. The French still call a British pound a *livre*. The slang term for a pound is a *quid* (see below).

queue   a line of people, usually waiting to pay for something. In shops you'll see a sign saying 'Please queue here'. It's what Americans call a 'line'.

quid   the slang term for pound/s – as in the unit of currency, not the weight. Always singular, as in 'Can you spare five quid?' or 'Twenty-five quid would do me fine.'

sale   a period when everything in the shop, or most things, have cheaper than usual prices. Shops put up posters saying 'Sale'. The *January sales* is the period after Christmas when many shops reduce prices to clear stock. The term *on sale*, however, is not used in this context – see *special offer*.

special offer   a term meaning an item has a cheaper than usual price. In other countries the equivalent is 'on special' or 'on sale', but in Britain if you ask whether an item is 'on sale', you're simply asking if it's available.

till   literally, this is the machine that calculates the prices and where sales staff put the money, but by extension it's the place where you pay. For example: 'You like that dress? Great. Let's take it to the till and get out of here.' Called the 'register' in US and Australian English.

CLOTHES

Visitors to Britain may see items advertised for sale and wonder what they are. Here are some peculiarly British terms for items of clothing, and a few other items, with their definitions or translations:

anorak   a hooded weatherproof jacket. The word comes, via Danish, from the Inuit word for a sealskin garment designed to protect the wearer from polar temperatures. The British version is made of cloth rather than sealskin, although some visitors might feel they need the original fabric on a cold wet day in London! (See page 102 for more fascinating *anorak* terminology.)

balaclava a close-fitting head and neck cover, which leaves just the face exposed. The word was adopted in Victorian times when British women made such head coverings for soldiers fighting through the frigid winter in the city of Balaklava (Ukraine), during the Crimean War.

braces a pair of elastic straps over the shoulders to hold up trousers; called 'suspenders' in the US. (*Suspenders* means something else in British English – see opposite.) See page 146 for more on **braces**.

cagoul a jacket, usually made of nylon and waterproof and breathable (thanks to a high-tech 'membrane' fabric attached to the nylon). Originally developed for hikers and outdoor enthusiasts, this type of garment is now worn by city types around town as well.

dressing gown what you might wear to cover your body or pyjamas between bedroom and bathroom, or just while getting properly dressed; called a 'bathrobe' in the US. In British English, the term refers to the silky or thick cotton variety.

fancy dress a character costume. If you're invited to a *fancy dress party* in Britain, you're supposed to come in your Tarzan get-up or your Dracula cape, not a morning suit or pink chiffon gown.

flip-flops rubber sandals with simple straps over or between the toes. Called 'thongs' in Australian English and 'jandals' in New Zealand English. (The term *thong* is used in British English, as it is in many other variations of English, to describe very skimpy briefs – usually worn by women. Once again, context is everything.)

frock a rather old-fashioned term for a smart dress

jacket for men, this means the top half of a formal suit or a blazer ('If I'd have known the president was coming I'd have worn a jacket and tie, instead of this T-shirt'). It also means a coat ('It's cold outside, you'd better wear your jacket').

jumper woollen sweater

knickers women's underpants

mackintosh raincoat; often shortened to *mac*

pants underpants (whether for men or women). In British English it does not mean 'trousers', as in the US or Australia. The word 'pants' is also a slang term for 'bad' or 'useless'.

suspenders technically, suspenders are the strips of elastic attached to a *suspender belt* which hold up *stockings* (see the box below), but the term is often used to mean 'suspender belt' ('I was standing there in my bra, pants and suspenders when some guy just strolled into the changing room').

trainers short for 'training shoes', meaning gym/tennis/ jogging shoes; often called 'sneakers' in US English and 'runners' in Australian English

trousers leg-wear for both men and women. These are what Americans call 'pants'.

vest in Britain this is a short-sleeved or sleeveless undershirt. A mother may say to children: 'It's cold today, so you'd better put a vest on.'

TIGHT FIT

The two pieces of fine female leg-wear that are held up by a suspender belt have historically been called *stockings* both in Britain and the US. When the nylon one-piece garments that cover the legs and lower torso came onto the market, Americans called them 'pantyhose', while the British called them *tights* – although the British term is also sometimes used in the US these days.

waistcoat a close-fitting, sleeveless, buttoned garment often worn under a suit or formal jacket, over a shirt. Called a 'vest' in the US.

Wellington boots high rubber boots; often shortened to simply **Wellingtons** or **wellies**. They were named after the Duke of Wellington (1769–1852), the great general and statesman who defeated Napoleon in the Battle of Waterloo. Although his boots were leather. They're also sometimes called **gumboots** (a term more familiar in other English-speaking countries).

British English is often mischievous and outrageous, and boasts a vast vocabulary of slang and colloquialisms. Some linguists estimate that British English contains around 20,000 slang terms (although many of these originate in America or other English-speaking countries), so it would be impossible to cover them all in this book.

Some slang words and colloquial expressions are widely used across Britain. Others are less well known, or only used in certain areas. In the same way, some colloquial words have been with us for centuries – the first recorded use of *booze*, for example, occurred in the 14th century, and the term *jet set* may derive from Chaucer's use of *jet* to mean 'fashion' in the *Canterbury Tales*. Other slang terms seem to be invented overnight, only to disappear from use just as suddenly.

This chapter is divided into three main sections: everyday slang and colloquialisms; street talk and less common slang terms; and swear-words and obscenities. For jargon popular in British workplaces – especially the office – and some terms from the world of politics, see the Lifestyle & Society chapter.

FAST-MOVING SLANG

The here-today-gone-tomorrow nature of some British slang terms was well illustrated in 2005 when British international long-distance runner Paula Radcliffe was competing in the London marathon, and unexpectedly needed to urinate. With no facilities nearby, she bravely ignored the presence of nearby spectators and a global TV audience and relieved herself in the open, then carried on running. For a few weeks, *doing a Paula* was the slang term for peeing in the gutter. A month later, the expression had fallen out of use, and is now (apart from this little reminder) totally forgotten.

Keep in mind that slang changes constantly, and even some of the phrases in this book may have fallen out of use by the time you read it. A great way to keep up to date is to browse or search through online resources. Websites also tend to come and go, but two long-standing and highly recommended sites are Urban Dictionary (www.urbandictionary.com) and the Dictionary of Slang (www.dictionaryofslang.co.uk). If they too have disappeared by the time you read this book, a search engine will undoubtedly locate others!

Everyday slang

Most linguists agree there's a distinction between slang and colloquial (ie informal) speech, but few agree on exactly where the distinction lies! Generally, slang is 'harder' – facetious, insulting, vindictive, or all three! – but there's a great deal of overlap between British slang and colloquial speech. Most of the terms listed in this 'Everyday Slang' section are acceptable in all but the most formal of situations; we've tried to indicate any that would be avoided in polite company.

aggro   trouble; violence; hooliganism; an argument; a fight. (From 'aggression' or 'aggravation', and often spelt 'agro'.) The word is used as a noun in British English; for example 'There was a lot of aggro when two rival gangs of football supporters met in the street.' It's not used as an adjective as in Australian English: Brits wouldn't say 'Don't be so aggro.'

argy-bargy   (pronounced 'ahjy bahjy') an argument; a fight; wrangling. As in 'There was a bit of argy-bargy down the pub last night – two blokes arguing over a pool match.' The term was used to great effect by tabloid newspapers in the 1980s when Britain went to war against Argentina over possession of the Falkland Islands.

ASBO/asbo   an acronym for Anti-Social Behaviour Order, an order introduced in 2005 to help police combat hooliganism and petty crime ('I was caught stealing from a shop, and had an ASBO slapped on me'). It has developed into a (lower-case) byword for a control device, as in 'This car is so powerful it doesn't just need good brakes, it needs an asbo' or 'The team played an aggressive match worthy of an asbo.' It also quickly became a verb: 'Steve's been asboed so he can't come out tonight.'

banger   an old car in poor condition

bangers   sausages

beeswax   business ('What I do with my money is none of your beeswax'). Sometimes spelt and pronounced 'biz-wax'.

beggar   pest, rogue, scamp, scoundrel. ('The little beggar hid my car keys' or 'George waited until it was my round before finishing his pint, the crafty old beggar'). Sometimes used as a more polite alternative to ***bugger*** (ie instead of 'crafty old bugger') and in those cases sometimes spelt 'begger'.

bent   corrupt or illegal. The word is also derogatory slang for homosexual.

bill   the police, as in 'Watch out, here comes the bill.' Also often ***the old bill***.

bless   short for 'bless them', or 'bless her'; normally used in the context of children or babies, meaning something like 'How sweet' or 'She's so cute.'

blimey   often combined with ***cor*** to form ***Cor blimey!*** – an expression of surprise. (Originally invented to replace the blasphemous phrase 'God blind me'.)

bloke   man (equivalent to 'guy')

bloody-minded   intentionally difficult; obstinate, persistent, stubborn

blotto   so tired as to be unable to think. Also means drunk ('I feel absolutely blotto').

bobby   police officer. The term comes from Robert Peel, the British Prime Minister who established the Metropolitan Police Force in 1828. Newspapers frequently call for 'More bobbies on the beat'.

bodge   an ineffective or poor-quality repair, as in 'The plumber came to fix my shower, but made a real bodge of the job, and it still leaks.' It's also used as a verb: 'I tried to bodge my broken exhaust pipe with a bit of wire, but it still fell off.'

bonk   to have sex. ('Don't go in there, Arthur and Sharon are *bonking*.') Hence also: *a bonk* (noun) and *bonked* (adjective) as in 'Sharon went home well and truly bonked.'

boob   colloquial term for mistake. (eg 'I asked if it was his daughter, but it was his girlfriend. I made a major boob there.')

boobs   colloquial term for breasts

BYE-BYE BONK

The word *bonk* (referring to sexual intercourse) seems to have first emerged in the 1970s, and appeared in newspaper headlines of the 1980s as a conveniently short and sanitary substitute for another relevant four-letter word. In the same way, the term *plonker* first appeared in a TV show, invented to take the place of a less acceptable (but similar-sounding) word for 'fool' or 'idiot'. Both *bonk* and *plonker* have now passed into everyday use.

At one time, however, *bonk* had a different meaning. Some endurance athletes, particularly racing cyclists, would talk about 'getting the bonk', meaning they were very tired due to extended exertion (in the same way as a marathon runner might say they were 'hitting the wall'). Hence, the wise cyclist would carry some food in a *bonk bag*. Now that *bonk* has another connotation (still connected to exertion though) the earlier meaning has largely dropped out of use.

botch to fail or make a mistake. 'I really botched my driving test.' Also used synonymously with *bodge* (see the definition opposite).

bottle bravery, courage. ('He doesn't have the bottle to ask her.') Hence, *lost your bottle* means you're scared.

brilliant cool, great. ('You should see my new trainers, they're brilliant.')

bum backside; buttocks. ('After driving all day, my bum was aching.') A much more acceptable term than *arse*; advertisements for a brand of soft toilet paper even feature the strapline 'Be kind to your bum.' *Bum* also means 'to borrow' or 'scrounge'; for example 'Can I bum a couple of quid off you?' or 'Can I bum a fag off you?' – the latter translating as 'Can you give me a cigarette?' in British English.

bumbag a small bag strapped around the waist; what Americans call a 'fanny pack'. See page 147 for a definition of *fanny* and an explanation of why the term 'fanny pack' isn't used in Britain.

bung this means 'put', as in 'Just bung it in the oven.' It also means 'give', as in 'do this for me and I'll bung a few quid your way.' As a noun, *bung* means 'a bribe', especially in a sporting context. A jockey might *take a bung* to hold a horse back and throw the results of a race, for example. In the 1990s, several major football matches were rigged after players received large *bungs*.

chat talk; gossip. 'Let's sit down and have a chat.'

chuffed delighted, pleased. Often used in the phrase *chuffed to bits*.

clever physically well, generally used in the negative: 'I don't feel too clever' means 'I'm sick'

cock-up error, mistake. This colourful compound word can also act as a verb ('Look what you did, you cocked up everything' or more often '… you cocked everything up').

crafty artful, clever, skilful; all with a slight implication of underhand behaviour

cropper failure. Often used in the phrase *come a cropper*, literally meaning 'have a bad fall' (possibly relating to horse-riding); metaphorically meaning a scheme has flopped.

daft silly; mildly crazy

dead extremely, very. For example, 'I went to that new club last night. It was dead good.'

dodgy (the *o* is pronounced as in 'hot') awkward; questionable; unreliable. ('I wouldn't buy that cheap watch: it looks dodgy.') Can also be used to describe a person: 'That Jimmy's always got the police calling round; he's a bit of a dodgy character.'

dole financial aid provided to the unemployed by the state. (Often called 'welfare' in other countries.) Being unemployed is hence often called being *on the dole*.

done cheated, tricked. ('I was done out of 20 quid.')

dosh (the *o* pronounced as in 'hot') money, cash

dotty feeble-minded, silly

drip a boring, uninspiring, weak or feeble person

end of story that's final, no more discussion. For example, 'If someone looks at me funny, I'll punch them, end of story' or 'If you don't do your homework, you'll go to bed without supper, end of story.'

fag cigarette. ('I'm just popping out for a packet of fags.')

fagged exhausted. ('After working a 12-hour shift I was completely fagged.') Also **fagged out**.

fair enough okay, I agree, that's acceptable. ('You said I was off work on Monday. Fair enough. But I worked overtime on Tuesday' or 'You want 250 quid for that old car? Fair enough, I'll take it.')

fiddle literally means 'to handle or play with using the fingers', often with negative connotations – 'I was fiddling with the computer and now it won't work' or 'Don't fiddle with your hair.' Hence, **fiddling about** has come to mean wasting time. **Fiddle** also means to cheat (to **fiddle the books**, for example, is to falsify the accounts).

flog sell

gob mouth, hence **gobsmacked** (meaning surprised, eg 'Little Sammy had refused to eat vegetables for years, so I was completely gobsmacked when he suddenly started wolfing them down.') Also **gobshite**, a vulgar term for someone who's cheeky, talks rubbish or simply talks too much.

grand one thousand pounds (money), as in 'That new car cost me 20 grand'

grass to inform (usually the police) about someone's misdeeds. Hence **grassed up** means to be informed on, as in 'I was grassed up and now I'm in prison.'

jammy lucky

kip a nap or short sleep

lad a boy. In the plural it can also mean adult (or teenage) friends: 'He's okay, he's one of the lads' or 'I'm going down the pub for a pint with the lads.' In the singular, **lad** often has connotations of mischievousness, and means something like 'wise guy' – as in 'I didn't do well in school because I was too busy being a lad.' A **lad's mag** is a magazine featuring, among other things, cars, music, computer games and pictures of scantily clad women.

laugh (often pronounced 'laff') Used as a noun, this can mean 'a good time', as in 'That party was a right laugh' or 'Let's go out and have a laugh.' **Having a laugh** can also mean 'joking', as in 'Are you having a laugh?' (meaning 'Are you serious?').

lolly money

lost the plot angry; confused; rambling; or all three. ('Then Jimmy lost the plot completely and started shouting at everyone in the pub.')

minder bodyguard

moolah money

naff tacky, unfashionable or uncool; ***naff off***, however, means 'go away'. See the box below for more.

ned hooligan, rowdy person, troublemaker. Possibly an acronym for 'non-educated delinquent'.

nick to steal. ('The kids decided to nick sweets from the shop'). It also means 'to arrest' (*Policeman:* 'If you touch

NAFF IS NAFF

The word ***naff*** was widely used in Polari – the 'underground' slang language favoured by gay British men in the 1950s and 1960s (although its origins are much older). The word is commonly defined as an acronym of 'not available for fucking' which came to mean generally unavailable and then simply 'bad' before crossing into mainstream slang and acquiring its current meaning – tacky, unfashionable or uncool. In reality, ***naff*** may be derived from the noun ***naffy***, meaning idiot or fool in some old dialects spoken in northern England, or from the Romany (Gypsy) word *naflo*, meaning broken or useless. People still remember Princess Anne shouting 'Naff off!' at a group of newspaper photographers, even though it happened in the 1980s. It's not clear if she knew the possible derivation of her outburst.

another drop, I'll nick you for drunk driving'), and *the nick* means the prison or the police station ('Take him down to the nick'). Thus, you might get a paragraph such as: 'A lad I know was nicking cars. Ended up getting nicked for it. Got taken down the nick, then did two years in Wormwood nick.'

nutcase   silly or crazy person; often shortened to *nutter*

over the moon   pleased, thrilled, very happy. Most famously used by football team managers on TV (*Interviewer:* How does it feel to win the match, Ron? *Manager:* Me and the boys are over the moon, Trevor).

pad   house or flat, as in 'This is a nice pad' or 'He lives alone in a trendy little bachelor pad'

ponce   ostentatious, effeminate or gay man. (The word *nonce* has a similar meaning.) Also, a lazy man living off his wife or girlfriend's earnings, and a verb meaning to borrow (usually inappropriately and permanently), as in 'He's always poncing money off me.'

potty   foolish, silly (but not as bad as 'crazy'), or very keen on something (eg 'she's potty about motorbikes')

as sick as a parrot   originally a phrase coined by football players to express disappointment on suffering a defeat; now a general term meaning 'sad' or 'dispirited' (but not 'ill')

skint   having no money (ie 'broke')

slippy   slippery (as in an icy surface); or quick and evasive ('We can't catch that thief, he's a slippy character')

Sloane Ranger   wealthy, well-connected young person, with the implication that they're also superficial and vacuous. Taken from Sloane Square, an expensive London shopping and residential district.

snog   to kiss passionately; *a snog* is a long passionate kiss. Especially used by/about teenagers; also used humorously ('Come here and give me a good old snog').

SUSPECT DEVICES

The slang word *suss* can be used in various contexts. If something is uncertain or someone unclear in their intentions they might be described as *suss* (from 'suspect' or 'suspicious'). The *suss law* was a controversial law permitting police officers to stop and search suspicious people (the controversy centred on *who* was considered suspicious). From that came *suss out*, meaning first 'to investigate' (as in 'Let's suss out that guy'), and then simply 'to check' or 'to follow up' ('We need to suss out the route in advance' or 'That's a good suggestion, I'll suss it out'). Someone who knows something or is generally well-informed was therefore said to be *sussed*, and from there *sussed* developed to mean 'properly organised' or simply 'good'. Thus, from being a pejorative word, *suss* has become a term of approval. It's now *well sussed!*

sort out   figure out; fix, straighten. For example, 'I'll get it sorted out' means 'I'll fix it'). Often shortened to simply *sorted* so 'It's all sorted' means 'it's all arranged' or 'it's all fixed'.

spondulicks   money, pronounced 'spondoolicks' (*sponds* for short)

spot   a portion, some. For example, 'a spot of tea', 'a spot of rain' or 'a spot of trouble'.

stumm   quiet (pronounced 'stum' or 'shtoom'). *To keep stumm* means 'to keep quiet'. (From German *stumm*, meaning 'mute', via Yiddish.)

take the mickey   to tease and/or humiliate (as in 'Don't take the mickey out of the way I walk. I can't help it, okay?' or 'Don't be offended, he's just taking the mickey'). The obscene (and more commonly used) version is *take the piss* – see the Swearwords and Obscenities section.

telly   television

tight   mean with money (eg 'Oh come on, lend us a quid, don't be so tight')

whinge (rhymes with 'hinge') to whine or complain. For example, 'All the baby did was whinge all night' or 'That meeting was a real whinge-session.'

willy penis. Unlike other terms for the male organ, this word is fairly harmless and can be used in all but the politest company.

wind up (pronounced to rhyme with 'mind') as a verb it means 'to annoy', as in 'That music really winds me up.' As a noun, **wind-up**, it means either 'an annoyance' or 'a trick' ('He said it was the Prime Minster on the phone, but I knew it was a wind-up.'). It does not mean 'to start' except in the context of clocks and watches.

wonga money

yob like **ned**, a hooligan; troublemaker; or rowdy person. Also **yobbo**.

GOING TO THE DOGS

Dogs are popular not only as pets in Britain but also for use in metaphors. A **dog's breakfast** is a mess or a weird mixture. The **dog's bollocks** is the opposite – it means great, top-quality, successful or the best, and is often shortened to **the dogs**, as in 'I went to that great new bar last night; it's the dogs.' (The **badger's nadgers** is preferred by some Brits. Both terms are coarse variants of the **bee's knees**.)

The amount of dog terminology in British slang can confuse foreigners. In the film *The 51st State*, for example, the American character played by Samuel L Jackson famously asks his British partner in crime 'Any dogs involved?'

Street talk

Young urban people speak perhaps the most flexible, vibrant and fast-moving varieties of British English. One of the most interesting aspects of the list of 'street talk' that follows is just how many words mean 'good' or 'cool'. A similar number translate as 'bad' or 'uncool'. It's so typical of the English language; one word would do, but why stop there?

Increasingly, the new slang terms young British people adopt come from Australian and American English – not surprising, given the international nature of TV, music and cinema. Thus, although we've tried to concentrate on British terms, some of those listed below will be familiar to Americans and Australians already.

bafta   good, cool

banging   enjoyable, fun ('We had a banging time last night'); in the context of music, loud and hard (eg 'banging techno')

Beemer   a BMW car

bender   drinking spree

black   good, cool

bling   ostentatious jewellery, especially on men. (Originally a term applied to the adornments favoured by rap artists, now more widely applied.)

blood   friend, mate (used predominantly by black youths in London). So 'Wassup blood?' (meaning 'What's up mate?') might be answered with 'Just hanging out with me bloods.'

boost   to steal a car ('Kev boosted a Beemer last night')

bruv   brother; meaning 'mate' (eg 'Wassup bruv?')

chav   a term referring to one of an entire subculture of white working-class teenagers, characterised by: poverty; ill health; low education; violence; vandalism; the wearing of fake sportswear and cheap jewellery; the driving of poorly customised second-hand cars; the prodigious consumption of alcohol, cigarettes and junk food; and early reproduction. It's vaguely similar to the US concept of 'trailer trash'. The term is thought to derive from an old Romany (Gypsy) word for 'child', which later became an insult for adults. Its widespread modern usage is partly due to the popularity of the website www.chavscum.co.uk, which claims to offer 'a user's guide to Britain's new ruling class'. **Chav** has spawned words such as **chavettes**, **chav-dom**, **chav-towns**.

class   good, cool; attractive

decent   good, cool; attractive

div   dork, fool, idiot. ('I feel such a div in this hat.')

doss   a noun meaning 'very easy' ('That exam – what a doss!'). Also a verb that means 'relax' or 'do nothing': 'I don't feel like going out tonight, so I'm just going to doss around at home.'

draw   marijuana

filthy   cool; extreme; wild. As in 'That tune's got some filthy bass on it' or 'We had a filthy time last night.'

fit   attractive, sexy

gaff   house, place to live (eg 'This is a nice gaff, mate')

gear   recreational drugs

geezer   this can mean simply 'man' or 'bloke' (eg 'Who's that geezer?'), or it can be used in place of 'mate' (eg 'Nice one geezer!'), or to mean something like 'hustler' or 'wheeler-dealer' (eg 'He's a bit of a geezer, always getting money from somewhere')

gross awful, disgusting; ugly

innit? (ie 'isn't it?') a phrase which seems to seek corroboration but is actually just a way to round off any statement. For example, 'I hate the way she wears her hair, innit?' or 'We went to London last weekend, innit?'

jissum/jissom good, cool

horizontal cool, relaxed, easy-going

kicking enjoyable, fun

large a big night; cool; fun. Especially said of a party or club (for example 'Bob's party was well large.'). Hence ***having it large*** or ***larging it***.

loved up high (usually on ecstasy)

lush good, tasty, attractive

messy generally used to meaning 'eventful' and involving lots of drugs/alcohol/trouble – eg 'Last night was messy, man: I downed a pint of vodka and woke up in the park.' Can also refer to the effects of drugs: 'I just smoked a massive joint and I'm feeling a bit messy now.'

minger (rhymes with 'singer') an ugly person

minging (pronounced to rhyme with 'singing') unpleasant; ugly

mint good, cool, nice; attractive

moose unpleasant, boring; ugly person

nugget a £1 coin

pants bad: used both as an adjective ('This place has no atmosphere – it's pants') and an expletive ('Oh pants!')

pillock idiot, fool

puff marijuana

A BIRD IN THE HAND …

British English slang words of yesteryear – still heard today in traditional songs – include *bird* and *bush*, meaning male and female genitals respectively, and shedding a whole new light on the phrase 'a bird in the hand is worth two in the bush'.

raasclart originally a Jamaican insult (possibly literally meaning 'arsecloth'); also used to describe black slang generally, especially as spoken by white wannabes. So someone might say, 'Look at those fucking chavs, giving it all that raasclart bollocks.'

rank disgusting, ugly

sad bad; unfashionable; unlikable. Often used as an insult; for example 'Sit down and shut up, you sad bastard.' The corresponding noun is *sadcase* or *saddo*.

safe excellent, cool

shandy someone who can't handle drink. (It's also a type of drink – see page 87 for more.)

sharp attractive; sexy; fashionable. Often used in a derogatory context: 'Never trust the guys in sharp suits.'

skank an unfashionable, badly dressed person. *To skank* is to steal or cheat.

skanky ugly, smelly, dirty, foul

skeg an unfashionable, badly dressed person

sketchy drugged out; flaky, unreliable

skunk strong cannabis

smart good, cool; fashionable

sorted good, cool; fashionable. Also, in the context of drugs, 'organised'. The guy outside the club might say, for example, 'You sorted for E's?' (ie ecstasy).

sound good, cool; fashionable

stomping enjoyable, fun

sucky dull, bad

tax steal

tightarse a person who's mean with money (not someone neurotic or anally retentive)

top excellent, cool; but also a verb *to top oneself* meaning 'to commit suicide' ('Life is so hard, sometimes I feel like topping myself')

twat an idiot (also an obscene term for female genitals). *To twat*, however, means to strike, hit or punch ('Shut the fuck up or I'll twat you').

twoc (pronounced 'twok') to steal a car and go joyriding (probably an acronym for 'take without consent')

well very. As in 'Let's go to Club X – the music's well good' or 'Don't annoy Billy, he's well hard.'

whatever all-purpose dismissal, in a conversation, of what the other person has just said

whizz speed (amphetamines)

wicked excellent, cool, exciting

SLANG EVERY-BLOODY-WHERE

As well as cropping up very frequently between 'normal' words, British swearwords sometimes crop up between syllables, as in *abso-bloody-lutely*, meaning 'yes, I agree', or *halle-fucking-lujah*, in the context of celebration ('We finally got a pay rise – halle-fucking-lujah'). A favourite we once overheard was 'This pub is dirty and packed full of *hoi po-fucking-loi*' – neatly combining a phrase derived from ancient Greek with an Anglo-Saxon expletive.

yard house (eg 'I got the gear back at me yard, man'). From Jamaican English.

There are dozens of slang terms not included here. Street slang in particular goes in and out of fashion so quickly that if you try some of the above expressions on a young British person they may laugh and say something like 'That's sooooo last year' or 'Yeah, like whatever, grandad.'

Swearwords & obscenities

Let's not ***beat about the bush*** – a lot of British English slang is obscene. It's usually best not to try out the words in this section in public! Having said that, what's considered unacceptable is constantly changing, and some expressions that were seriously obscene or blasphemous at one time have now become, if not acceptable, at least far less shocking.

The list below provides explanations or equivalents for a small selection of British obscenities. (If you want to know more, try searching the two websites mentioned at the start of this chapter.)

arse backside. Brits also use ***ass*** (as Americans do), which tends to be regarded as less offensive than ***arse***. ***To kick ass*** means to 'get things moving' (or in some contexts, to be successful, eg 'Man United played a kick-ass game and won five-nil'; ***a kick up the arse*** means something like 'a reprimand' or a 'wake-up call'. The word ***arse*** also gives us ***arsehole*** (idiot; unpleasant person) and ***arse-licker*** (lackey, yes-man). The phrase ***can't be arsed*** means 'can't be bothered' (eg 'I intended going to go into town tonight, but now I can't be arsed').

bastard   originally someone of illegitimate birth but now a general insult, as in 'Look at the damage you've done to my car, you stupid bastard'

bleeding   same meaning as **bloody** (see below) but slightly less offensive. ('You want to borrow my car? Not bleeding likely.') It was possibly originally a euphemism for **bloody** or another blasphemous term – perhaps 'Bleeding Heart' – when these were considered genuine swearing.

bloody   an all-purpose slang term, generally used for emphasis. So if the train was **bloody late**, it means it was very late, and if someone calls you a **bloody idiot** they mean something like a 'big idiot' or 'stupid idiot'. *He can bloody well wait* amounts to 'He can damn well wait', while *Not bloody likely* means 'very unlikely'. This swearword has its roots in medieval blasphemy: it was initially 'beloved lady' (ie 'I swear by/on the Virgin Mary').

Bloody hell!   exclamation which is used to mean anything from 'Damn it!' to something milder like 'Wow!'

bollocks   a vulgar term for testicles ('I was playing football and got kicked in the bollocks'), but also used as a general way to disagree with a statement: *Tom:* 'Are you scared?' *Harry:* 'Am I bollocks.' (It's the equivalent here of 'Am I hell.') Likewise, 'That's a load of bollocks' means 'That's rubbish.'

bugger   originally this meant 'to have anal intercourse', but it's now a relatively inoffensive all-purpose insult (eg 'Don't leave it there, you stupid bugger.'). It's also used to express surprise ('Well bugger me!') and in phrases such as 'Buggered if I know/care' (ie I don't know/care) or simply as a stand-alone expletive: eg 'Oh bugger!' instead of 'Oh fuck!', but not quite as bad. *To bugger* is also used to mean 'to break', 'foul up', 'ruin' or 'spoil' ('The engine's buggered'), and *I'm buggered* means 'I'm exhausted.' If someone tells you to **bugger off** they mean 'Go away!'

bugger all   nothing ('He's got bugger all in the bank' or 'I give bugger all what you think')

crap slang for faeces (eg 'some bastard let their dog leave a big pile of crap on my lawn') but generally used to mean poor quality or simply bad ('I bought a new pair of boots down the market, but they were crap'), or to express disagreement (John: 'I can earn 500 quid a day cleaning cars'. Jim: 'That's crap' – ie, that's rubbish, that's untrue). It is generally not used as an expletive ('oh crap, I'm late for work') as in American English.

cunt slang for the female genitals, and one of very few swearwords in British English to retain its full offensive power in most situations. It's used mainly as an insult, as in 'Some cunt's gone and nicked my car' or 'Come here and say that you little cunt.' Hence ***cunted***, ***cunting*** and ***cuntish***. In London and southern England particularly (where it's pronounced 'cahnt'), ***cunt*** is used almost as multifunctionally as ***fuck***. However, it can also be used affectionately between blokes and ***geezers*** (eg 'Go and get the beers in, ya big cahnt').

fuck of Anglo-Saxon origins, ***to fuck*** is to have sex (also ***to have a fuck***; and ***a good fuck*** is someone good in bed). It also means 'broken' or 'ruined' ('All my plans were fucked by this idiot') or 'drunk and/or in trouble' ('After 17 pints of lager, I was totally fucked last night'). Then there's ***fuck up***, ***fuck off***, ***fucked off***, ***fuck all***, ***fuckwit***, phrases like ***Fuck me*** or ***Fuck it***,

WHAT THE FUCK?

It seems the British have been notoriously foul-mouthed for centuries – around 1400 Joan of Arc was calling the English *les goddams*. By the 1960s the French were calling the Brits *les fuckoffs* thanks to the large number of British people who base their conversation on the words *fuck* and *fucking*, with the occasional *wanker* or *bastard* thrown in for variety. Those at the cutting edge seem to be moving towards a Zen form of British English in which *fuck* will be the only word – shaped, nuanced and spat out to convey every thought and sentiment.

and a lot more besides. ***Fucking*** is most commonly used either to mean 'very' ('I had a fucking brilliant holiday') or simply to replace 'er' and 'um' (see the box on the previous page).

knackered   tired, worn out

pissed   drunk (not 'angry', as in American English)

pissed off   angry

piss-up   drunken session ('We had a great piss-up on Saturday night'); a variation is ***on the piss*** ('We had a great night on the piss on Saturday')

roger to have sex with, usually with implications of rough behaviour or unwillingness on the part of one partner. Also used (as with ***fucked*** and ***buggered***) to mean 'broken' or 'damaged': 'Thanks to the way you drove my car, the gearbox is completely rogered.'

shag to have sex; slightly less vulgar than ***fuck***. ***Shagged*** is also slang for 'tired' or 'worn out'.

shit faeces. ***To shit*** is thus 'to excrete'. Also a widely used slang term in British English meaning 'bad' ('That film was shit') or 'a bad person' ('Come here and say that, you little shit'). Also an expletive (eg 'Oh shit, here come the cops', whereas North Americans might say 'Oh crap…').

shithouse toilet (often used in the phrase 'He's as tough as a brick shithouse')

the shits diarrhoea (as in 'I got a bad case of the shits while travelling in India'); 'having the shits' doesn't mean 'angry' or 'annoyed' as in Australian English

sod a derogatory term derived from 'sodomy', but which now means something like 'idiot', 'fool', 'jerk' etc. ('I saw you switch the cards you crafty little sod.') It's even sometimes used with a touch of affection: 'George had to work all night to get the job done, poor old sod.'

Sod off! Go away!

Sod it! Damn it!

spunk sperm. This word and its derivatives – ***spunky***, *a spunk*, ***got some spunk*** – is very rarely used in the contexts of bravery or sexual attraction, as it is in some other forms of English.

tosser fool, idiot. Used in a similar way, and has the same literal meaning, as ***wanker*** (see below), although it's less harsh. ('Get yourself off home, you silly old tosser.') A variation is ***tosspot*** ('You've had too much to drink, you tosspot'). The phase *I don't give a toss* means 'I don't care'.

wanker fool, idiot. Depending on the context it can be a severe or mild insult: you might say 'You're a bunch of fucking wankers' to a group of rival football fans, but then you might say 'Come on mate, don't be such a wanker, she's not worth crying over' to a friend. (Derived from the word ***wank***, literally meaning 'masturbate'.)

DRUNK AGAIN …

Believe it or not, all the expressions below are slang words or regional terms for being drunk. Last night I was …

arseholed, battered, bevvied, bevvied up, bladdered, blootered, bollocksed, bricked, buckled, buttwhipped, cabbaged, canned, creamed, crushed, cunted, floored, foetal, fucked, guttered, hammered, hamstered, kalied, kaly, lashed, leathered, leery, legless, mashed, monged, mortal, mortalled, off it, off my face, off my trolley, out of my face, out of my head, out of my tree, pallatic, para, paralytic, pished, pissed, pissed as a fart, pissed as a newt, pissed up, plonked, rat-arsed, ratted, reeling, scoobied, shedded, shitfaced, slashed, slaughtered, slewed, sloshed, sozzled, steaming, stotted, tanked, tankered, tired and emotional, trashed, trolleyed, twatted, wankered, wasted, wazzed, well gone, wellied, wrecked

And while we're on the subject, here are some choice expressions for vomit or vomiting:

barf, blow, blow chunks, blow your groceries, boak, chak, chuck, chunder, flurg, heave, hurl, lose your lunch, pavement pizza, praying to the porcelain god, shouting down the big white telephone, razz, retch, spew, technicolour yawn, throw, throw up, vom, yak

Isn't British English a delightful language? These words just roll off the tongue, don't they? Rather like the experience they describe …

This chapter looks at some words that appear the same in Britain and in other places where English is spoken, but which have different meanings in everyday use. There's also a small selection (there are many more!) of common words, phrases and expressions which have no direct equivalent in other versions of English, or simply need to be explained.

If you happen to find yourself in conversation with British-English speakers, knowing some of these terms will help avoid misunderstandings – and sometimes outright confusion.

Confusing terms

bandage   a strip of material for binding up a wound. The little stick-on things called 'bandages' or 'Band-Aids' else-where are called ***sticking plasters*** or simply ***plasters*** in Britain.

billion   the British 'billion' is a million million (unlike the American 'billion', which is a thousand million)

bothered   worried, concerned. Most commonly used in the negative, as in 'I'm not bothered where we go', meaning 'I don't care where we go.' Or for example: *Jim:* 'Your girlfriend's left you.' *Jack:* 'I never liked her anyway, so I'm not bothered.'

LOOK WHO'S TALKING

In British English, a sentence is started with the word ***look*** to give it a strong emphasis, usually during an argument ('Look, I've said we're not going and that's final'). Speakers of Australian English who use ***look*** to start any sentence often seem unnecessarily forceful, and even aggressive, to British friends or colleagues.

braces   in British English these are elasticated straps used for holding up trousers, called 'suspenders' in America. The wire for straightening teeth, which Americans call 'braces', is called *a brace* in British English.

bum   colloquial term for 'backside' or 'buttocks' (see page 127 for more). It's rarely used to mean 'tramp' or 'hobo', as in American English, although *bumming around* (meaning 'doing nothing') is used in British English.

chemist   pharmacy or pharmacist. In other varieties of English, the word 'chemist' is usually applied to people who work in chemistry (in British English, for clarity, they might be called 'industrial chemists' or 'research chemists').

clever   in standard British English this means 'bright' or 'intelligent'. It doesn't mean 'shrewd', 'sly' and 'cunning' as in American English. When the British speak of a *clever* student, they mean simply a good student, not one who has figured out how to get a string of A grades without opening a book.

cot   a bed for a baby; a 'crib' in US English. What Americans call a 'cot' is sometimes called a *camp-bed* in British English.

consultant   a high-ranking medical specialist such as a cardiologist, gynaecologist or paediatrician

dear   expensive ('This coat was dear, but it will last me for years')

ASIA'S A BIG PLACE …

The term *Asian* in British English generally refers to people from (or whose ethnic origins lie in) the subcontinent of India, Pakistan and Bangladesh. It generally does not refer to the whole continent of Asia. For clarity, someone from Kyrgyzstan, for example, might be called a *Central Asian*; people from China or Singapore and the surrounding nations are known as *East Asian* or *Southeast Asian* as appropriate.

decorate in British English, to ***decorate*** a room involves painting the walls or putting up new wallpaper. It does not mean getting new curtains, carpets or furniture.

diary a personal journal or an appointment book

dumb mute (not 'stupid' as elsewhere)

fanny in British English this is a mildly vulgar term for vagina. It does not mean 'buttocks', as in the US.

fight a physical confrontation, such as a boxing match or a scuffle in the street; not just an argument as in American English

flog to sell goods, usually of a shoddy or questionable nature ('He was caught flogging stolen CDs at the market'). As in other forms of English, it also means 'to whip', hence the expression ***flogging a dead horse*** meaning doing something pointless.

funny as well as 'humorous', this also means odd, unusual, or unexpected in some way

funnily oddly; usually used in the phrase ***funnily enough*** ('I said I'd see him down the pub, but funnily enough he wasn't there')

graft hard work, usually manual, with implications of poor reward. There is no implication of illegal or underhand activity in this word in British English.

homely of a place, to be domestic, comfortable and welcoming. It does not mean 'plain-looking', and the American equivalent 'homey' isn't used in Britain.

knickers women's underpants (not knee-length trousers)

mad insane (not 'angry' as in American English)

momentarily in British English this means *for* a short period of time, not *after* a short period of time as in American English. A British person might say, for example, 'I glimpsed the rainbow momentarily, then it was gone.' To British ears, an American receptionist saying 'I will deal with your query momentarily' implies a very abrupt service.

no question no possibility, out of the question. If the British say, 'There's no question of troops being sent in' they mean 'There's no chance of troops being sent in.' To other speakers of English, the phrase could mean 'There's no doubt of troops being sent in.'

odd strange; or occasional. When a British weather forecaster says, 'We may get the odd shower', she doesn't mean the one that looks a bit strange. It means there may be a few showers throughout the day.

purse a very small bag to keep money in. This tends to be a feminine term: men keep their money in a **wallet**. The larger bag in which a purse and other items like keys may be kept (which is called a 'purse' in American English) is called a **handbag** in Britain. If it's slightly smaller and has no handle or shoulder strap, then it's called a **clutch bag**.

randy in America this is a male first name, but in British English it means 'sexually aroused' (or 'arousing'). The US equivalent is 'horny'.

rubber a pencil eraser, but also a slang term for condom, hence schoolboy giggles and cries of 'too late' in response to the art-room request 'I've made a mistake, can I borrow your rubber?'

smart chic; fashionable; of neat appearance. Also, but less commonly, used to mean 'intelligent', as in American English.

HAIR TODAY, GONE TOMORROW

If you go for a haircut in Britain, note that hair cut short over the forehead is called a **fringe**, not 'bangs' as in US English. Also, what the Brits call a **hair grip** is called a 'bobby pin' in US and Australian English.

BEWARE THE SHITS

Two colloquialisms common in Australia have very different meanings in British English. First, *spunk* is rarely used to mean 'an attractive person' or 'brave': it's a vulgar term for 'sperm'. Second, *the shits* does not mean 'angry' or 'annoyed': it's slang for 'diarrhoea'.

stop colloquial version of the word 'stay'; as in 'Don't stop in the sun too long' or 'I packed a bag and stopped overnight at John's place.' Serious misunderstandings can arise when *stop* is used in phrases like 'Sorry I'm late – I stopped talking at Rita's place' which means the exact opposite of how it sounds.

surgery clinic where patients see a family doctor (not a hospital doctor). Also, a place where Members of Parliament meet constituents individually.

table to raise or discuss a topic; to put a topic on the agenda. In Britain, *tabling* an issue is not the same as *shelving* it (ie postponing it).

tip to dump; a rubbish dump and by extension any untidy place. A parent might say to a messy teenager, for example, 'This room's a tip.' In some country areas there are signs that read 'No Tipping', meaning 'don't dispose of rubbish here'.

venue location, site, place of meeting. In the US, the word 'venue' is commonly used in the field of law, designating where a trial will take place. In Britain, it's used in daily conversation ('We've changed the venue for departure tomorrow morning – we'll meet in the car park instead of at the hotel.') As in the US and some other countries, *venue* is also used in the context of entertainment; a club's promotional flyer, for example, may invite you to 'Enjoy dance and trip-hop at one of the coolest venues in London'.

wild angry, as well as (of an animal) undomesticated. Hence the old joke, '*Interviewer:* You're tame now, but were you wild when you were captured? *Gorilla:* Wild? I was furious!'

Miscellaneous words & expressions

This section lists some common words, phrases and expressions in British English which have no direct equivalent in some (or all) other versions of English spoken around the world. Others are included here simply because they might be unfathomable to other English-speakers.

acclimatised accustomed to one's surroundings; 'acclimated' in American English

antenatal before birth; normally used in a medical context, as in 'Pregnant women receive good antenatal care in this hospital'

anti-clockwise the opposite of 'clockwise'; called 'counter-clockwise' in American English

at the end of the day in the last analysis; ultimately

bank holiday public holiday (ie a day when banks, as well as shops, close)

bit a small part. The British say 'Which bit would you like?' (which part would you like?) and 'It fell to bits' (it fell apart) and 'Gather up all these bits' (gather up all these parts). It's also a colloquial term for genitals (especially female genitals), as in 'The gynaecologist examined all my bits'.

bits and bobs assorted items, odds and ends

brilliant great, terrific. The equivalent of 'awesome' in some other varieties of English.

budgerigar a type of small parrot, a popular pet in Britain (***budgie*** for short)

carry on to continue (as in 'Turn left, then carry on down the road for a mile'). A ***carry-on*** is also a disturbance or unruly happening ('There were two neighbours fighting in the street last night – what a carry-on.') or a mix-up or an effort. 'We had to go to four restaurants before we could find a table – it was a right carry-on.'

carry the can hold responsibility, take the blame. For example: 'If that plan goes wrong, it'll be you that carries the can.'

case short for suitcase

chap informal or fond term for man ('He's a nice old chap')

cockerel, cock male chicken (a 'rooster'). ***Cock*** is also a slang term for 'penis' – handy for schoolboy double entendres.

cuddle embrace, hug. The British tend to say 'Give me a cuddle' rather than 'Give me a hug.'

direct action a protest in the form of a march, strike or sit-in

donkey's years a very long time

drawing pins small pins with a flat head, for attaching paper to a notice board; 'thumb tacks' in American English

drop if you go to a party in Britain and the host asks if you'd like a drop of wine, don't expect a miniscule quantity – they'll bring you a glass of the normal amount

early days too soon to know: 'Conditions at the factory are set to improve, but it's early days. We'll know for sure later this year.'

early doors colloquial term for 'early'. (It originates from the period when pubs could open only at certain times of day. If a pub opened earlier than usual the locals celebrated 'early doors'.)

effing and blinding swearing excessively

fall out a disagreement: 'I've had a fall out with my sister, she said my kids are ugly.' Also ***to fall out***: 'I've fallen out with my sister …'

fancy   imagine; like; be attracted to. So: 'Fancy that!' (Imagine that!); 'He fancies himself as quite a lover' (He thinks he's quite a lover); 'Do you fancy a walk on the beach' (Would you like a walk on the beach?); 'Nick fancies Sue' (Nick is attracted to Sue).

fête   (pronounced 'fate') a fair held to raise money for a charity, school, church etc

get your own back   get even with, get revenge

go   turn. ('It's your go to throw the ball.')

gone missing   lost, disappeared (eg 'The cat's gone missing.')

gone off   when referring to food, ***gone off*** means 'to have spoiled' (eg 'The meat's gone off'). In general conversation, it means 'to have lost interest' (eg 'I've gone off the idea').

grasp the nettle   be brave and take hold of the situation. (Equivalent to 'take the bull by the horns' or 'bite the bullet'.)

hard done by   unfairly dealt with

hire   rent, as in 'I won't go by train, I'll hire a car.' The words ***hire*** and ***rent*** are often used interchangeably in British English.

FLOORED

In Britain (and many other European countries), the bottom floor in a multistorey building is called the ***ground floor*** and the floor above is the ***first floor***. In the US, these would be called the 'first floor' and 'second floor' respectively – all the floors in a British building are labelled one number lower than an American would expect. The sight of a confused American never fails to amuse the locals, leading some US visitors to suspect that the numbering is part of a sinister conspiracy to throw them off guard.

in the event in the end; in the final instance. In British English, this phrase doesn't need to be followed by 'that', as in 'In the event that (something happens) …' It can simply mean 'the actual outcome' (eg 'We were going to spend our holiday in Greece, but in the event we just stayed at home').

in the first instance in the first place

jam tomorrow a common expression in Britain meaning that if you do without something today, you'll be rewarded tomorrow (or sometime later)

jolly very ('That's jolly decent of you')

ladybird flying insect with a red, black-spotted body; a 'ladybug' in US English

last but one the second last, penultimate

layabout malingerer; person who doesn't attempt to find work

lead (pronounced 'leed') a length of rope or leather used for walking a dog; 'leash' in American English

life assurance an insurance policy on your life (a policy on your house or car is just 'insurance', as in the US)

lift a mechanism for carrying people between floors in a large building; an 'elevator' in American English

look after take care of (someone or something)

lot group of people; faction ('You don't want to fall in with that lot.')

meant to supposed to, should ('It's a joke, so you're meant to laugh.')

midges gnats; tiny mosquitoes

miss out omit ('I missed out three people on the invitation list for the party.')

muck dirt. In the US, 'muck' is sludge – something moist and decomposing. In Britain, it isn't nearly so odious, it's just another word for dirt of any sort. Thus, where Americans would say something is 'dirty', the British might say it's **mucky**.

net curtains filmy curtains that go between the heavier curtains and the window; 'sheers' in American English

next door but one two doors away (usually used to mean two houses further along a street)

not half very (eg 'He's not half funny', meaning 'He's hilarious'). Often used to express agreement (eg *Jim*: Is that CD good? *Alan*: Not half, mate).

not on not right, won't do (eg 'You're always late – it's just not on')

nouse (pronounced to rhyme with 'house') common sense; intelligence. For example: 'He's keen but he hasn't got the nouse for this job.'

on about talking, often with implications of excess (eg 'What's that guy on about this time?')

one-off single occurrence (whether planned or accidental)

over the top too much; overdone

over the way across the street

pack it in quit; finish (eg 'We've done enough work for today, let's pack it in' or 'Jimmy, stop kicking that ball, I've told you already to pack it in')

parky cold (eg 'The wind's got up so it's a bit parky outside')

peckish   hungry (for a snack)

pensioner   someone who gets a government age pension; by extension, any older person (usually aged over 60 or 65). Also called a **senior citizen**.

persons   people. In a formal context, the British often use **persons** as the plural of 'person'.

PMT   premenstrual tension (PMS in other countries)

post   letters. 'Mail' in American English.

punters   colloquial term for the general purchasing (or betting) public, as in 'Every Saturday this place is full of punters looking for bargains'

put paid to   put an end to, finish off (often mispronounced as 'put pay to')

redundant   to be **made redundant** is to be dismissed from a job because the factory closed or the position became obsolete. It's not the same as 'fired' or 'sacked', which imply dismissal for reasons of incompetence. Hence, a **redundancy**: 'The steel works closed with 2000 redundancies.'

remit   (pronounced with the stress on the first syllable: 'remit') a committee's scope, directives, or terms of reference when examining a question or carrying out a commission. For example, 'We can't do any hiring or firing – it's not within our remit.'

roll-up   roll-your-own cigarette

row   (pronounced to rhyme with 'how') a quarrel or argument. **To row** means 'to argue'. For example, 'They had a row'; 'They've been rowing about it.' In Britain this word is used commonly even for mere disagreements, whereas Americans only use it for a really furious, noisy confrontation.

sacked   fired

sanitary towels   'sanitary napkins' in other varieties of English

scupper to defeat. This is a naval term – originally meaning to sink an enemy ship – which has crept into everyday British speech. So you might *scupper* someone's plans, or your own plans might be *scuppered*.

sell-by date expiration date marked on food products. *Past its sell-by date* is a popular expression in Britain for anything (such as an idea or fashion) that's passé or out-of-date.

serviette napkin

sick vomit (verb and noun). Americans 'throw up'; the English *are sick*. The result of the regurgitation is also called *sick*, as in 'I had to scrub the carpet because there was sick all over it.'

skip a large metal receptacle for carrying away rubbish, for example after building work. A 'dumpster' in American English.

skive colloquial word meaning 'shirk' or 'evade a duty'. Hence *skiver*, meaning 'lazy person' ('He's a bit of a skiver, never around when there's work to be done'). When combined with *off* it implies slinking away, as in 'The boss wasn't around so the guys skived off and went to the pub.'

smellies colloquial term for scented toiletries such as bubble bath and soap

spanner a 'wrench' in American English (an *adjustable spanner* is a 'monkey wrench' in the US)

stick short for 'walking stick'; a 'cane' in American English

stone a unit of weight, equivalent to 6.3kg (there are 14 pounds in a *stone*). Used by most Brits when discussing their own weight. Generally used in the singular: 'I could run faster, but at 15 stone I'm carrying a lot of weight' or 'I lost two and a half stone after going on that diet.'

straight away immediately

takeaway ready-to-eat food (eg 'Let's get a Chinese takeaway tonight')

tearaway juvenile delinquent, wild teenager, hooligan

terry towelling cotton fabric of uncut loops. Called 'terry cloth' in US English.

time and time again frequently. Americans might say 'time and again', but in British English there's an extra 'time'.

torch portable electric light ('flashlight' in American English)

treble three times. It's commonly used when giving numbers in Britain. For example, '41222' might be said 'four one treble two'.

undertaking a promise or assurance (eg 'They gave us the undertaking that they'd do it free of charge')

value in the US, when you want to sell your house, you get it appraised: in Britain, you get it *valued*

vet to check (something). All kinds of things can be *vetted*: a scheme to be launched, the quality of someone's work, a candidate for a job ('To join the police you have to be positively vetted'). *Vet* is also short for *veterinarian*.

way forward the best way to proceed; the right thing to do. It's often used in a business context, but not always: 'I used to take my boyfriend sailing, but he hated getting wet. That wasn't really the way forward, so I took up cycling instead and now we do things together.'

wind flatulence. Hence **breaking wind**; and babies with bloated stomachs are said to have **trapped wind**.

wool in Britain, any yarn used for knitting – whether acrylic or genuinely from a sheep's back

work out calculate, figure out (eg 'Let's work out the cost of a week's holiday in Spain')

MAKE A DATE

The British write their dates in a day/month/year order; the first day of March in the year 1968, for example, would be written **1st March 1968** (or **1/3/68**). The same date would be 'March 1st, 1968' (or '3/1/68') in the US.

Also, the Brits don't say '1st March through 5th August', meaning 'up to and including the 5th', but simply **to the 5th** – it's understood that the 5th is included. Other British English phrases connected to time and dates include:

fortnight	a two-week period (deriving from 'fourteen nights')
half-four	four-thirty (and 'half-two', 'half-three', etc)
Thursday week	a week from Thursday (so 'Tuesday week', 'Sunday fortnight' and so on)

English is spoken in many different ways throughout Britain, and some regional dialects can be mind-boggling for outsiders. Take, for example, the word for a small meal or snack. Depending on where you are in Britain this might be called your:

baggings	*dew-bit*	*nummet*
bait	*docky*	*nunch*
beaver	*dowen*	*nuncheon*
bite	*drum-up*	*progger*
biting	*jower*	*snap*
biting-on	*lowance*	*snapping*
bitings	*minning-on*	*tenner*
clocking	*nammet*	*tenses*
crib	*nammick*	*tommy*
crust		

Here's another example; across Britain, regional terms for 'left-handed' include:

banh-handed	*gammy-pawed*	*kippie-fisted*
clicky-handed	*gawky-handed*	*pally-fisted*
corrie-fisted	*kack-handed*	*scrammy-handed*
corrie-flug	*kaggy-handed*	*scutchy-fisted*
cuddy-wifted	*kecky-handed*	*skerry-fisted*
cue-handed	*keggy-handed*	*skiffy-handed*
cutchy-handed	*kerrie-fisted*	*watty-handed*
dollock-handed	*kervag*	
galley-handed	*key-handed*	

A few of the terms in the second list have fallen out of use since the 1960s, but in some areas the suffixes *-pawed*, *-fistit* or *-klookit* are used instead of *-handed* or *-fisted*, giving even more options. Some have taken on the extra meaning of 'clumsy'. There are more examples in each chapter in this book – see, for example, the different ways of saying 'hello' and 'goodbye' on page 30 – the range and variety of regional terms is incredibly broad.

The other key feature of British English is the number of regional accents: even when the words are the same, they're pronounced very differently in different parts of the country. An inhabitant of Glasgow, for example, might have genuine difficulty understanding someone from rural Devon (and vice versa) when they're both using standard English expressions, before even getting on to any local dialect terms.

Visitors to Britain who speak English as a first language are often surprised when they experience difficulties communicating with people speaking in a regional dialect. Then, just as they're getting *the hang of* (used to) the dialect, they travel 50 miles (about 80km) down the road and are faced with a whole new set of words and pronunciations.

What's even more remarkable is that all these variations exist in a comparatively small area: Britain measures less than 1000 miles (under 1600km) from north to south, with an area only slightly larger than the US state of Pennsylvania or New Zealand's North Island.

What's a dialect?

Most linguists agree that a regional dialect has three facets:

1. *Specific words* (that aren't used elsewhere). For example, *jag* is used in parts of Scotland to mean a medical injection, but out of context this would not be understood in other parts of Britain.
2. *Sentence structure*. In northern England, for example, the positions of pronouns or prepositions are sometimes different to those in Standard English. *I'll bring it you up* means 'I'll bring it up to you.'

3. ***Accent***. That is, the way words are pronounced (whether they're local or standard English terms). For example, in southwest England the sound *s* is often pronounced more like a *z* (as in ***Would you like beer or zider?***), while in London and the Southeast the letter *t* is frequently dropped from the middle of words and replaced with a glottal stop.

The terms 'dialect' and 'accent' are often used interchangeably, but this is misleading. Standard English can be spoken with a regional accent. When different words and sentence structures are used as well as the accent, *then* it's a dialect.

It's also important to note that the accents and dialects covered in this chapter are just regional varieties of English. Several other distinct languages are also spoken in Britain (Welsh, Scottish Gaelic and so on), and these are discussed in more detail in the following chapter.

Britain's linguistic regions

For the rest of this chapter we'll look at some of the varieties of English spoken in the various parts of Britain. Starting in London and the southeast of England, we'll work westwards and then northwards through the rest of England, looping through Wales and finishing in Scotland.

Please note that the divisions we've used in this book are fairly sweeping. In reality, there are many areas within each region that have their own accents and dialect terms, subtly different to those of their neighbours. In Wales, for example, the accent of the English spoken in the city of Cardiff is different to the accent of Swansea around 30 miles (around 50km) along the coast. And both the city accents are different from the accent found in the farming lands of mid-Wales, and different again from the accent of the former mining valleys of South Wales. The experts can even tell the individual valley dialects apart; someone from Glynneath apparently has a slightly different lilt or turn of phrase to someone from the Rhondda area just 10 miles away. All fascinating stuff, but unfortunately it's beyond the scope of this book to cover each tiny area in detail.

GIVE US A BREAK

Many English dialects use a plural pronoun where the singular would normally be used, especially dialects in the north and Midlands. For example: *our kid* (my child), *our mam* (my mother), *our lass* (my wife), *give it us* (give it to me), *Do you really love us?* (Do you really love me?).

The word *us* is also often used where 'our' would appear in standard English. *Give her us best wishes* means 'Give her our best wishes'. Other examples:

We'll come down the park after us dinner.
This is us new house.
We're just trying to better us-selves.

And so on. You get the picture.

Bidialectal bliss

Don't be put off by the sometimes bewildering words and phrases in this chapter. If you happen to be travelling around Britain, or if you meet a Brit travelling in your country, and you genuinely can't understand their local dialect, say so. Someone from an area where a donkey is called a *pronkus*, for instance, will almost always know the word 'donkey' as well. With the exception of a few elderly people who might find translation of this kind more difficult, most people are 'bidialectal' and can switch from their local dialect into standard British English, and will soften their accent as well for the sake of the weird foreigner who keeps saying 'Pardon?'

London & the Southeast

The accents and dialects of English in London and the Southeast are closest to what most non-British people will think of as typical English accents. They come in three principal flavours:

- the speech of the establishment and the middle and upper classes, known as *Received Pronunciation* (*RP*), and also called *BBC English*, *the Queen's English*, *Oxford English* or simply *posh English*
- the working-class variety known as *cockney*
- an intermediate accent, falling somewhere between RP and cockney, called *Estuary English*, as it's spoken in the region around the estuary of the River Thames

RECEIVED PRONUNCIATION

Received Pronunciation (RP) needs little explanation. Think of English actors Hugh Grant in the film *Love Actually*, Patrick Stewart in *Star Trek: the Next Generation* or Emma Thompson in practically anything, and you've got the general idea.

London & the Southeast

NORTH SEA

The Wash

ENGLAND

King's Lynn
Norwich
Great Yarmouth
Lowestoft
Peterborough
Ely
Huntingdon
Cambridge
Newmarket
Bury St Edmunds
Bedford
Haverhill
Ipswich
Woodbridge
Banbury
Milton Keynes
Sudbury
Colchester
Felixstowe
Witney
Aylesbury
Luton
Stevenage
Baintree
Oxford
St Albans
Harlow
Chelmsford
Abingdon
Hemel Hempstead
High Wycombe
Watford
Newbury
Reading
Windsor & Eton
LONDON
Southend-on-Sea
Basildon
Rochester
Sheppey
Margate
Chatham
Ramsgate
Maidstone
Canterbury
Guildford
Sevenoaks
Ashford
Deal
Crawley
Royal Tunbridge Wells
Dover
Horsham
Folkestone
Rye
Strait of Dover
Chichester
Lewes
Bexhill
Brighton
Hastings
Bognor Regis
Hove
Seaford
Eastbourne
Isle of Wight
FRANCE

English Channel

0   40 km
0   20 mi

REGIONAL VARIATIONS

- Southeast England
- London
- Britain

GREAT BRITAIN

Received Pronunciation was originally just one regional accent among many, and in fact originated to the north of London in the English Midlands. It became the accent of power and privilege as London grew in importance over the years. From the 18th century onward, wealthy families became ashamed of their regional accents and wanted to distinguish themselves from the local *yokels* (peasants, country bumpkins), and RP spread across the country. Today, it's widespread throughout Britain – sitting alongside regional accents in most areas – and is spoken especially by the upper classes.

You'll frequently hear that RP is the 'best', 'clearest' and 'most beautiful' accent of English, but these views are based on prejudice against other accents as much as anything. Increasingly, people in the south of England are moving away from RP speech because of its associations with old-fashioned class-based snobbery, and are turning instead to the accent midway between RP and cockney which has become known as Estuary English.

ESTUARY ENGLISH

Estuary English developed quite recently: linguists generally agree that it's only been around since the late 1970s or early 1980s. It's perceived as an 'everyman' accent – not posh like RP, but not as 'common' as pure cockney, although it uses features of both.

The popularity (and importance) of Estuary English is such that British leader Tony Blair – among several other politicians – used Estuary pronunciations in his speeches of the 1990s. This included introducing glottal stops into phrases such as 'a better Britain' so it came out more like 'be-er Bri-un' – the *t* is replaced with a sound like the one between 'uh' and 'oh' in 'uh-oh'.

This technique is particularly interesting, as until the 1960s (or even later) politicians from beyond London would often drop their regional accents in favour of RP in order to be accepted by their colleagues. In contrast, Mr Blair's natural accent is close to RP and it seems he roughened it a little so as to appear more of a 'man of the people'.

COCKNEY

Traditionally, a true cockney is someone born within the sound of Bow Bells – the bells of the church of St Mary-le-Bow in the heart of London – but these days the term is more loosely applied to people from anywhere in London, and cockney is the name of the predominant accent of the entire city and surrounding area.

Key features of cockney pronunciation include the heavy use of glottal stops instead of the letter *t* in words like 'butter', 'Battersea' or 'lottery' and the dropping of *h* at the beginning of words like 'hurry', 'Harry', or 'Hampstead Heath' (in cockney, *Amsted Eeth*). The letter *l* can often sound like *w*, as in *miwk* for 'milk'. The *r* sound also becomes more like a *w* so that 'free', for example, can often sound like *fwee*. The *th* sound in words like 'thought' and 'mother' are replaced with *f* and *v*, making these words sound like *fort* and *muvva*.

Cockney is probably best known for its *rhyming slang* – in which everyday words are replaced by words or phrases that rhyme with the original. Thus 'feet' become *plates of meat*. In many cases, however, just the first part of the slang phrase is used, so the slang for 'feet' is *plates* (eg 'These new shoes are killing me plates'). Sometimes the spelling of the slang term changes slightly too. For example, the slang for 'hat' is *tit for tat*, but this gets shortened to *titfer*.

There are numerous theories on the origin of rhyming slang. It could be something to do with thieves needing a secret language that the police couldn't understand. It could be just

---

MODERN COCKNEY

Relatively recent additions to the rhyming slang lexicon include *Daily Mail* for 'tale' (as in 'I don't believe a word of his daily') and *Harvey Nichols* for 'pickles' ('You got any Harveys to go with this cheese?'). Another recent addition is *Britney Spears* for 'beers', giving us sentences like 'Go and get the Britneys in.' Author and TV commentator Melvyn Bragg has also seen his name became part of today's vocabulary, though perhaps not as he might have wished!

a way of confusing all outsiders. If the latter, it still works – especially as new rhyming slang words appear all the time (see the box on page 166). Some of the more modern terms, though, seem a touch *skinned* (*skinned alive* – contrived).

Below is a selection of cockney rhyming slang. It may seem long and confusing, but don't worry – the average Londoner doesn't use very much rhyming slang in day-to-day conversation, and when it is used the meaning is usually clear from the context.

airs and graces	braces
apples and pears	stairs
April Fool	stool
Aristotle	bottle
army and navy	gravy
Artful Dodger	lodger
Auntie Ella	umbrella
babbling brook	crook (ie thief)
bacon and eggs	legs (often shortened to *bacons*)
ball of chalk	walk
Barnaby Rudge	judge
Barnet Fair	hair (always shortened to *barnet*)
bat and wicket	ticket
Bath bun	sun
bees and honey	money
beggar my neighbour	labour
boat race	face
Bo Peep	sleep
bow and arrow	sparrow
bread and butter	gutter
bread and cheese	sneeze
Brussels sprouts	scouts
bubble and squeak	beak (meaning 'magistrate')
bucket and pail	jail
burnt cinder	window
Burton on Trent	rent (shortened to *Burton*)
bushel and peck	neck
butcher's hook	look (shortened to *butcher's*)
Cain and Abel	table
Cape of Good Hope	soap

Captain Cook	book
cash and carried	married
cat and mouse	house
china plate	mate ('How's it going, me old china?')
cobblers' awls	balls ('It's a load of cobblers')
cock linnet	minute
cock sparrow	barrow
country cousin	dozen
currant bun	son
daisy roots	boots
dickory dock	clock
dicky bird	word
dig in the grave	shave
dog and bone	phone ('Get on the dog and call us a taxi')
dustbin lid	kid
elephant's trunk	drunk
field of wheat	street
fife and drum	bum
fisherman's daughter	water
frog and toad	road
gay and frisky	whisky
ginger beer	queer
Glasgow Ranger	stranger
goose's neck	cheque
Harry Randall	candle
holy friar	liar
Isle of Wight	right
Jack Jones	alone ('I'm all on me Jack tonight')
Jimmy Riddle	piddle
Joanna	piano ('Let's have a tune on the old Joanna')
Khyber Pass	arse
Lillian Gish	fish
loaf of bread	head ('Don't be daft, use your loaf')
merchant banker	wanker
mince pies	eyes
monkey's tail	nail
Mother Hubbard	cupboard

Mutt and Jeff	deaf (often shortened to *Mutt an'*, which sounds like 'mutton')
north and south	mouth
Oliver Twist	fist
on the floor	poor
Oxford scholar	dollar
peas in the pot	hot
pen and ink	stink ('That cheese pens a bit')
pimple and blotch	scotch
plates of meat	feet
pleasure and pain	rain
pony and trap	crap
pork pies	lies (shortened to *porkies*)
rabbit and pork	talk ('He was rabbiting on for hours')
raspberry ripples	nipples
read and write	fight
Richard the Third	turd
rub-a-dub-dub	pub
salmon and trout	stout (ie beer)
Scapa Flow	go ('Quick, let's scarper')
Sexton Blake	cake
skin and blister	sister
stand at ease	cheese
tiddly wink	drink
tin flute	suit
tit for tat	hat
Tom and Dick	sick
Tom Thumb	rum
weasel and stoat	coat
weeping willow	pillow

COVER YOUR MINCE PIES

Political correctness hasn't had much effect on rhyming slang – the term *trouble and strife* is still used for *wife*. And it doesn't shy away from vulgarity either – a woman's *Bristols* are her breasts (*Bristol City* is a football team, thus *Bristol Cities* equals *titties*). On the other hand, it's also used to euphemise: *love a duck* is rhyming slang for a popular expletive.

The only problem with understanding rhyming slang is if the rhymes are for British slang words. So a cockney might – at least in theory – be heard to say:

> I don't **Adam and Eve** it. I went out to get some **Uncle Fred**, a **linen draper**, and some **oily rags**, but when I reached for my **sausage and mash** I found a **teapot lid** had fallen out of my **Lucy Locket**. So now I'm totally **hearts of oak**!

Some of that should be fairly obvious – 'I don't Adam and Eve it' means 'I don't believe it'. But **oily rags** are **fags** (cigarettes) and a **teapot lid** is a **quid** (one pound). In this case, outsiders have no hope!

Southwest England

The southwestern part of England is generally held to mean the long arm of land extending from the counties of Hampshire, Wiltshire and Gloucestershire through Somerset and Dorset to Devon and finally Cornwall. This region is called by some the **Westcountry** (one word) or the **Southwest Peninsula** – especially once you get west of Bristol.

The far western reaches of this region are almost as distant from London as the northern counties of Cumbria and Northumberland, and as a result the local speech has remained distinct and features of much earlier forms of English are still evident.

In addition, the English spoken in Cornwall features some words from Cornish, a Celtic language related to Welsh and Breton. Examples are **clicky-handed** ('left-handed', from Cornish **glikin**, 'left'), and **whidden** ('runt' or 'weakling', in a litter of pigs for example – from Cornish **gwyn**, meaning 'white'). The word **fossick** ('to search or root around', as in 'She was fossicking around in my sock drawer') is also Cornish in origin but now used in other parts of Britain.

Southwest England

English Channel

- Basingstoke
- Andover
- Winchester
- Salisbury
- Southampton
- Portsmouth
- Ryde
- Isle of Wight
- Bournemouth
- Poole
- Weymouth
- Dorchester
- Shaftesbury
- Stonehenge
- Warminster
- Swindon
- Cirencester
- Cheltenham
- Gloucester
- Chippenham
- Bath
- Bristol
- Wells
- Glastonbury
- Yeovil
- Lyme Bay
- Minehead
- Taunton
- Exeter
- Exmouth
- Torquay
- Torbay
- Tiverton
- Ilfracombe
- Barnstaple
- Barnstaple Bay
- Okehampton
- Launceston
- Tavistock
- Plymouth
- Bude
- Bodmin
- Wadebridge
- Newquay
- Truro
- Falmouth
- Penzance
- Land's End
- Mount's Bay

ENGLAND

Cotswolds

WALES

Cambrian Mountains

St George's Channel

Cardigan Bay

St Brides Bay

Gower Peninsula

Bristol Channel

Lundy

CELTIC SEA

GREAT BRITAIN

0   40 km
0   20 mi

Legend:
- Southwest England
- Britain

ACCENT

The features of the accent of southwest England include a pronounced r sound and a drawn-out a sound – so words like 'farmyard' are doubly affected. The i tends to sound more like oi, as well – the word 'tie' is pronounced more like 'toy'. The sound s often becomes z, such that the county of Somerset is jokingly spelt 'Zummerzet'. The th sound, too, is often pronounced d, so you might hear **Dat's de end of my story** or possibly words like **dree** (three) and **droat** (throat). Another feature is the occasional switching of sounds, so that 'crisp' is **crips**, 'clasp' is **claps**, 'rich' is **urch**, and 'red' is **urd**.

The southwest accent is invariably adopted by other Brits when they're trying to imitate a farmer or country bumpkin: **Oo aar, oi loikes zoider, oi does**, goes the old routine. This stereotype actually goes back a long way. In Shakespeare's King Lear, for example, Edgar, the son of the Earl of Gloucester, has disguised himself as a peasant and adopts an appropriate accent:

> **Ch'ill not let go, zir, without vurther 'casion … Good gentleman, go your gait, and let poor volk pass. An chud ha' bin zwaggered out of my life, 'twould not ha' bin zo long as 'tis by a vortnight.**

The first word **Ch'ill** (meaning 'I will') comes from 'Ich will'. Despite its German appearance, using **Ich** for 'I' was quite common in southwest parts into recent times. You'll also notice that the s has become z (**zir, zwaggered, zo**), and f has become v (**vurther, volk, vortnight**), both still features of southwestern English today.

CELTIC PENGUIN?

There's a theory that the word 'penguin' (referring to the flightless seabird of the southern hemisphere) derives from the Cornish or Welsh pen gwyn, meaning 'white head'. It's thought that the term was originally applied to another flightless aquatic bird, the now-extinct Great Auk of the North Atlantic, which looked a bit like a penguin.

Among the dialects of southwest England you'll also occasionally hear remnants of older forms of English grammar, such as *be* and *bist* meaning 'is' and 'are' (so *he be* means 'he is'; *ee bist* means 'you are') and *baint* meaning 'won't'. The word for 'him' is *er* and for 'them' is *mun*, as in *Er knawed mun well* – 'He knew them well.'

And finally, a habit unique to the southwest – especially in and around Bristol – is dropping the *l* from the end of words and adding an *l* where originally there wasn't one. So 'mangle' and 'mackerel' become *mango* and *macrow*, and 'idea' becomes *ideal* (*What's the big ideal?*).

VOCABULARY

The southwest is of course a very large region, and there are many variations within it. The rural accent of Wiltshire is different from the accent in Cornwall, for example; the urban accents of Bristol or Plymouth are different again. The examples of dialect words that follow are drawn mostly from Devon English, but can usually be found across the southwest.

argify	(pronounced 'argiffeye') argue
assards	backwards
auncy	(pronounced 'aunsee') anxious
bay-spittle	honey (lit: 'bee-spit')
bird	term of endearment to people of either sex
braksis	breakfast
caal	think (eg *What do ee caal you'm doing?* – 'What do you think you're doing?')
casn	cannot
dane	red-haired man
drumbledrane	bumblebee
emmet	ant
galley	to frighten, alarm (*Did er galley you?* – 'Did he frighten you?')
girt	great (ie large)
grockle	holidaymaker; visitor
grubbish	hungry
kaky	sticky

laceing	huge
lacer	huge
mort	a lot (*There's a mort o' volk up church* – 'There's a lot of people up at the church')
pitching	settling of snow
pluff	unwell
power	a lot
shrammed	(to be) cold
shug	shy
sketchy	strange, odd
spun out	angry
suent	smooth
tempt	touch (*Doant ee tempt it!* – 'Don't you touch it!')
woppit	a blow (*Er geed un a woppit roun yurrole* – 'He gave him a hit round the earhole')
yucks	hiccups

THE SOUTHWEST

The Westcountry habit of adding an *L* to the end of some words has resulted in a name-change for the region's largest city. It was originally called *Bristow* – from 'Bridge-stow', meaning a crossing on the river where boats tied up and unloaded – but the *L* was added and *Bristol* eventually became the official name and spelling.

A long-standing joke tells of three Bristol sisters called Evil, Idle and Normal. (Get it?) And confusion can result when Bristolians ask US visitors, 'What's life like in a miracle?' (Say it out loud, and it starts to make sense.)

West Midlands

As the name suggests, the Midlands is the central part of England. It's divided into two parts, the East Midlands and the West Midlands: the West Midlands is centred roughly on the city of Birmingham.

The Midlands

0 ────── 40 km
0 ────── 20 mi

NORTH
SEA

IRISH
SEA

Pennines

Whitby ○
Scarborough ○
Bridlington ○

Ingleton ○
Settle ○
Skipton ○
Ilkley ○
Keighley ○
Bradford ○   ● Leeds
Halifax ○
Huddersfield ○

Thirsk ○
Ripon ○
Harrogate ○
York ○
Selby ○
Beverley ○
Hull ●

Doncaster ○
Scunthorpe ○
Grimsby ○

Sheffield ○
Worksop ○
Gainsborough ○
Bakewell ○
Chesterfield ○
Lincoln ○
Skegness ○

Stoke-on-Trent ○
Derby ○
Nottingham ○
Newark ○
Boston ○
The Wash

Oswestry ○
Shrewsbury ○
Telford ○
Stafford ○
Loughborough ○
Melton Mowbray ○
Spalding ○
Lichfield ○
Stamford ○
Wolverhampton ○
Walsall ○
Leicester ○
Dudley ○
Birmingham ○
Coventry ○
Ludlow ○
Kidderminster ○
Warwick ○
Rugby ○
Northampton ○
Worcester ○
Stratford-upon-Avon ○
Royal Leamington Spa ○

Hereford ○

WALES

Cotswolds

ENGLAND

Grantham ○

■ The Midlands
■ Britain

GREAT BRITAIN

Birmingham (known fondly as *Brum* by the people who live there) is the second-largest city in Britain after London. Despite its size and its importance to the national economy, its inhabitants (known as ***Brummies***) tend to get something of a bad press – and it's all thanks to their accent.

ACCENT

One of the key features of the West Midlands accent is vowels which are 'lowered' – so 'me' sounds like 'may', and 'you' is pronounced *yow*. The words 'right' and 'price' are *roit* and *proice*, while 'fate' and 'tame' can sound more like 'fight' and 'time'.

The vowel in words like 'it' and 'bit' is more drawn out into an *ee* sound, so they sound like the words 'eat' and 'beat'. The *s* sound becomes something between a standard *s* and a *z*: 'bus' is pronounced more like *buzz*. Also, as in many urban accents of British English, most of the time *h* is either dropped from the start of words altogether or softened (so that 'home', for example, becomes more like *whum*).

Surely, there's nothing intrinsically unattractive about this accent. The negativity about it probably has more to do with the negative perceptions of the heavily industrialised West Midlands region. But then, Brummies themselves will pay their accent a backhanded compliment by saying that it's beautiful compared to the one in the area near Birmingham known as the *Black Country* (Dudley, Walsall, Wolverhampton). The Black Country folks, in response, say that Brum is just a watered-down version of the 'true' Midlands dialect.

Variations of the Brummie accent also can be heard in the rural – and very picturesque – counties of Staffordshire, Warwickshire, and Hereford & Worcester, which surround the urban West Midlands.

VOCABULARY

The expressions below may be heard generally around the Midlands, but especially in Birmingham and the Black Country.

adrenchen	soaking wet
am	is, are (hence *you am*, *we am* – usually shortened to *we'm* – and *am ya?*)
anent	against; next to
bab	baby, love, darling (as an endearment)
backen	to delay; to keep back
bad	ill
bin	am (*I bin* – I am)
bist	are you (eg *Weer bist?* – Where are you?); probably a shortening of *be thee* or *bin thee*
bonk	small hill (see *tacky-bonk*)
Bostin!	Great! Super!
caggy-handed	left-handed
cass-handed	left-handed
chunter	mutter or mumble; grumble
clammed	hungry
clemmed	hungry
cob	bread roll
cob it	throw it away
cod	to joke, to tease (*You'm coddin' me!* – You're joking!)
coost	could you (the negative is *coosn't*)
cost	can you (the negative is *cosn't*)
croggin' in	jumping the queue

West Midlands

cut	canal
donnies	hands (perhaps from French *donner*, 'to give')
fittle	food
frizoggled	freezing cold
gain	handy, skilful
got a nark on	annoyed (also *got a monk on*, *got a bag on*)
jed	dead (hence *jeth*, 'death')
lief	as soon as
mash	to brew (eg *the tea's mashing in t' pot*)
noggin	a thick piece (usually of bread)
pail	to beat (*I'll gi im a good pailin' when e comes whum*)
peg it	run away
pikelet	(two syllables: 'pike-let') crumpet
pither	potter about aimlessly
playing t'wag	playing truant
potch	forestall
powk	sty on the eye
reesty	(second syllable rhymes with 'sea') rancid (of fat, butter or cheese)
saft	silly, daft (so a *pack o' saftness* is a load of nonsense)
shommock	walk with a shuffling gait
skraze	graze, scratch
starving	cold (not 'hungry')
suck	sweets, candy
tacky-bonk	pit mound, slag heap (see *bonk*)
taff	to steal (perhaps from *Taff*, a nickname for a Welshman)
Tararabit	(pronounced 'tara a bit') Goodbye
weld	to hit someone
welly	nearly (eg *I was welly clemmed to jeth*)
wench	a girl (not derogatory, and used by both men and women)
wozzer	Birmingham term for someone from the Black Country
yawl	bawl; shout; cry loudly
yawp	bawl; shout; cry loudly
zowk	yelp; cry out

East Midlands & Yorkshire

The East Midlands is made up of the counties of Nottinghamshire and Derbyshire, centred on the cities of Derby and Nottingham, and sometimes includes Leicestershire as well. Further north is the large county of Yorkshire, containing the cities of York, Sheffield and Leeds.

Combined, this is a very large region, and so of course there's a good deal of variation in speech patterns. The accents of Leeds and neighbouring Bradford are slightly different from that of Sheffield. The rural accents are different again – people from the hilly Dale country or the coastal areas have their own subtle speech variations, which reflect the isolation of smaller towns and villages. But there are some common aspects too, and this section gives an overview of the basics.

BRASS IN POCKET

A famous Yorkshire mantra is **where there's muck there's brass**, meaning 'wherever there's dirt, there's money to be made' – a reference to the coal mines and factories that (in the past) thrived across the region. The correct northern pronunciations of the *u* (oo) and *a* (as in 'gas') sounds are essential. Say it with a southern accent and the locals may think you're a bit *nesh*.

ACCENT

The first thing most people notice about the accents of Yorkshire and the East Midlands is the vowels. Words like 'pass' or 'grass' rhyme with 'gas', rather than with 'farce', and 'water' may rhyme with 'batter'. The *u* in words like 'duck' or 'luck' is pronounced like the *u* in 'put'.

As in London and the Southeast, *h* is generally not pronounced at the beginning of a word, so that Yorkshire people will talk about going to **Ebden Bridge** or **Arrogate** instead of

'Hebden Bridge' and 'Harrogate'. (In fact, the latter is often pronounced *'arra*gut'.) You'll hear Yorkshire folk dropping the word 'the' and using instead a short *t* sound, so that the expression 'I put the baby in the car' might sound like *Ah put babby int car*. The letter *t* often turns into a *k*, so that 'little' and 'bottle' are pronounced *lickle* and *bockle* in some areas.

The Yorkshire habit of using *thee* and *thou* (usually pronounced 'tha' as in *Dost tha want some snap?* meaning 'Would you like some food?') can be found elsewhere in northern England. In other English-speaking countries *thee* and *thou* might seem quaintly biblical, but they're actually just a relic of earlier forms of English, in which 'you' was formal and 'thou' informal (like *tu* and *vous* in French).

> ## LOVE A DUCK
>
> The term *love* is widely used in the East Midlands and York-shire. Don't get the wrong idea if you ask a Yorkshireman the time and he responds, 'Half-twelve, love.' Said to a woman, it's the equivalent of 'dear' or some other innocuous term. Said to a man, it's like 'pal', 'mate' or 'buddy'. *Duck* is used in a similar way, but is more usually (though not exclusively) addressed to women.

VOCABULARY

As in many other regions, there's a wealth of dialect vo-cabulary in the East Midlands and Yorkshire. Some of the more common expressions are listed below.

allus	always
any road	anyway (also sometimes said *any road up*)
atta	are you (from 'art thou')
aye	yes
bap	bread roll
beck	small stream
bonny	fat, plump (not, as in northeast England and Scotland, 'attractive' – avoid saying 'Oh, you look so bonny in that dress' in Yorkshire!)

breadcake	bread roll
butty	sandwich
cack-handed	left-handed (or clumsy)
chab/chabby/ *chavvy*	child, baby
coursey	pavement (ie 'sidewalk' or 'footpath beside a road' in other countries)
dale	valley
gen	gave (the *g* pronounced as in 'get')
gen backword	go back on one's word (*He said he'd be there at the pub but he gen backword and never arrived*)
gennel/ginnel	alleyway; narrow path; passage between houses
gid	past tense of *gen*
Give over	(pronounced 'gee owa') Stop it; Be quiet
gob	mouth
hacky	dirty
happen	maybe (*Happen it'll rain tomorrow*)
lak	play (eg *Yon lad were lakin' in t'ginnel* – 'That boy was playing in the alleyway')
lass	girl; woman
loppy	dirty
lugs	ears
manky	dirty
mardy	grumpy
neb	nose
nebbin/nebby	nosy
nesh	soft, weak
nowt	nothing
owt	something; anything
right	very (*It's right cold today*)
selt	past tense of 'sell' (*I selt my car yesterday*)
semt/sempt	past tense of 'seem' (eg *the baby was ill in the morning but semt all right by dinner time*)
	(*Selt* and *semt* are common in Derbyshire, but less so in Yorkshire.)

sheggy-handed	see *cack-handed*
siling down	raining heavily
Sithee?	See you (ie 'Goodbye')
Sithee?	Do you see? (ie 'Do you understand?')
skinny	tight-fisted, mean
skrike	cry
sock on	fast asleep
starving	cold

WAIT A WHILE

A word of warning – watch out for the Yorkshire *while*. It doesn't just mean 'while' in the usual sense, it can also mean 'until': shopkeepers, for example, will tell you they're open 'nine while five'.

The story of the Yorkshireman who came to a *level crossing* (a crossing over train tracks) and was run down by a train after obeying the sign 'Do not cross the line while the lights are red' may be a tall story, but it's a good way of remembering this important distinction!

Northwest England

Lying between North Wales, the West Midlands and the Scottish border, with the coast of the Irish Sea on one side and the Pennine Hills on the other, is the northwest part of England. It includes the counties of Lancashire and Cumbria, the famous cities of Manchester, Liverpool and Carlisle, and the great countryside of the Lake District.

ACCENT

To the untrained ear, the accent and dialect of the rural areas of the northwest can sound similar to those of Yorkshire, County Durham and Northumberland, on the other side of the Pennines. (There are certainly more similarities between the northwest and northeast than there are between, say, the northwest and the southwest of England.) Certainly, many of the vowel sounds are the same, such as the short *a* – 'path', 'grass' and 'fast' have the same vowel sound as 'mat'. The *oo* in 'book', too, is pronounced in both areas rather like the *u* in 'chute'.

But don't let these similarities fool you. If you get a Lancastrian confused with someone from Yorkshire you could be in trouble: the rivalry between these counties goes back at least to the Wars of the Roses in the 15th century.

Cumbria is often said to be England's most beautiful county, thanks to its lakes and mountains and the lack of any large towns or cities. Although in previous centuries this was a major slate-working region, its rugged terrain and remoteness has helped preserve some speech forms from much earlier times. For example, the words *thee* and *thy* ('you' and 'your') are still used. Another is *dost* or *dust*, meaning 'do you?' as in *Dust come frae Ambleside?* (Do you come from Ambleside?)

Just to the south of Cumbria and the Lake District is Lancashire. The broad Lancashire dialect has the vowel sounds outlined earlier, along with features such as pronouncing 'asking' like *aksin*, 'bowls' as *bohwels*, 'water' as *watter*, 'wash' as *wesh* and 'wrong' as *rang*.

The biggest city in Lancashire (although these days it's a metropolitan area in its own right) is Manchester, and it's home to a very distinct dialect known (like the inhabitants) as Mancunian, or simply *Manc*. The best way to get an idea of the

COUNTING SHEEP

The dialectologist Peter Wright collected a huge number of expressions and pronunciations from Cumbria into a book called *Cumbrian Chat: how it is spoke*. In the book Dr Wright laments the extinction of the 1400-year-old Celtic-based number system used for counting livestock in Cumbria. From one to ten went *yan, tyan, tethera, methera, pimp, sethera, lethera, hovera, dovera, dick* then through *bumfit* (15) and up to *giggot* (20).

Northwest England

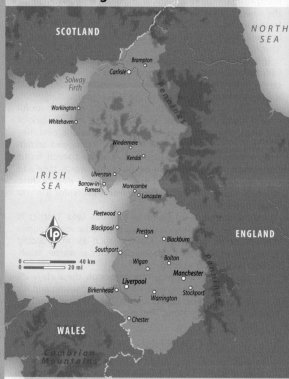

SCOTLAND

NORTH SEA

Brampton

Carlisle

Solway Firth

Pennines

Workington

Whitehaven

Windermere

Kendal

IRISH SEA

Ulverston

Barrow-in-Furness

Morecambe

Lancaster

Fleetwood

Blackpool

Preston

Blackburn

ENGLAND

Southport

Wigan

Bolton

Manchester

Liverpool

Stockport

Birkenhead

Warrington

Chester

WALES

Cambrian Mountains

Pennines

0   40 km
0   20 mi

Northwest England

Britain

GREAT BRITAIN

Manc accent is to watch a few episodes of the long-running TV soap opera *Coronation Street*, which is set in Manchester.

Not far from Manchester is Liverpool, home of the most distinct accent in the Northwest, and one of the most distinct accents in the whole of Britain. Liverpool's dialect is known as *Scouse* and Liverpudlians are known as *Scousers* (the name is said to derive from *lobscouse* – a mutton stew – which itself is almost certainly a nativised form of the German dish *Labskaus*). Scouse has been heavily influenced by Irish English, since so many Irish immigrants have settled in the city. Its distinctive features include replacing *th* at the start of words like 'those', 'things' and 'there' with the consonants *t* or *d*, so a sentence sounding like *What are dose tings dere?* isn't unusual. And *t* itself can often sound like *s* in Scouse, so that 'what' can sound like *woss*.

Some words from standard English have been combined, most famously *gis*, from 'give us', meaning 'give me' (eg *Gis a job*). The *k* sound in 'back' gets a guttural *ch* pronunciation, winding up like German *Bach*. And 'fur' and 'fair' often sound alike in Liverpool – but just to confuse the issue, sometimes Scouse 'fair' sounds like *fur* (to rhyme with 'stir') and sometimes 'fur' sounds like *fair* (to rhyme with 'stair').

TASTY!

Don't be surprised if someone asks you if you'd like a *shag* in Cumbria – it's local dialect for a sandwich.

VOCABULARY

Here's a very small section of words from the northwest:

bally-wart	stomachache
barmcake	bread roll (sometimes shortened to *barm*)
beawnt	going to
brid	a child (from 'bird')
camp	chat

chuck	term of endearment (as in the greeting *Ey up chuck*)
cob on	annoyed (*E's getten a cob on*, meaning 'He's annoyed')
collops	lots of
estin	dustbin
ey lads ey	reality, basics (eg *When it comes to ey lads ey* meaning 'In reality')
fain	glad
fratch	argue
frimbles	nervous, uncertain
giggle-gaggle	passage between houses
ginnel	see *giggle-gaggle*
hoo	she
jannock	reasonably good
keawer	sit
Lanky	Lancashire, or an inhabitant of that county
lish	agile; fit
mardy	grumpy; moody
moggy	in West Lancashire, a mouse rather than a cat!
moither	annoy
nazzy	bad-tempered
po fagged	exhausted
pownd	stressed (*A'm pownd t'deeath*)
shive	slice of bread
sken	to look
sneck	nose
tara	goodbye
utch	to move
wick	quick; agile; heaving with (*Wick wi' mice*)

Northeast England

Northeast England consists mainly of County Durham and Northumberland. We're now in the territory of the *Geordies* and the *Makems*, the natives of the cities of Newcastle-upon-

Tyne and Sunderland, a great urban area known collectively as Tyneside. The Geordie dialect spoken in the northeast is said to be among the most difficult to understand in Britain.

To some outsiders the Geordie accent sounds similar to a Scottish accent – and there is a direct influence, as Newcastle is close to the border and throughout history has attracted Scottish immigrants. However, in many instances, visitors from overseas don't realise that local people are speaking English and think it's Russian, say, or Danish. In fact, Danish visitors to Newcastle often seem to have an easier time understanding Geordie than some native English-speakers; the strong Scandinavian influence in Tyneside has persisted since the days of the Vikings.

Don't let this worry you! If you look blank when a Geordie says, *How pet, gannin' doon toon wi' wuh?* he or she will probably repeat it as 'Hello mate, do you want to go into town with us?'

ACCENT

A key feature of the Geordie accent is the pronunciation of vowels. The *o* sound often becomes *ee*, so that 'no' and 'do' are pronounced *nee* and *dee*. The word 'take' becomes *tak*, 'make' becomes *mak*, while 'all' becomes *al* or *aa'*, and 'walk' becomes *waak*. Similarly, the word 'know' is *naa*, 'stone' is *steeyen*, 'shirt' is *shawt*, 'cold' is *caad* and 'work' is *wark* – almost like the pronunciation of 'walk' in standard English.

CANNY CODE

In his book *Up North: travels beyond the Watford Gap*, Charles Jennings tells a story about the British forces campaigning in North Africa during World War II. Everyone had to use code when communicating by radio – except the Geordie regiments. As Geordies were unintelligible to most other native English-speakers, the reasoning went, the Germans wouldn't have a hope.

Northeast England

SCOTLAND

Berwick-upon-Tweed

Holy Island

Farne Islands

Wooler

Alnwick

NORTH SEA

Cheviot Hills

Haltwhistle

Newcastle-upon-Tyne

Tynemouth

South Shields

Sunderland

Pennines

Durham

Hartlepool

Darlington

Middlesbrough

ENGLAND

Northeast England

Britain

GREAT BRITAIN

The word 'out' is **oot**, and a 'house' is **hoose**; note that there's no h-dropping in Newcastle. In fact, sometimes an h is added to words such as 'away' (meaning 'let's go'), giving the classic Geordie call to arms: **Haway the lads!**

Comedians have long taken advantage of the potential confusions caused by these vowel differences. There's a story about a Geordie with an injured knee who goes to see his doctor. The doctor applies a bandage and asks, 'Now then, do you think you can walk?' The Geordie looks at him in amazement, and exclaims, **Wark? I can hardly waak!** ('Work? I can hardly walk!').

In parts of Northumberland people may be heard using the 'Northumbrian burr', a throaty r sound just like the one in German in words such as braun, produced in the back of the mouth. Also, often the sound ow comes out as oo: Newcastle brown ale, the city's iconic beverage, for example, is called **Newcastle Broon**. For some of the best written Geordie, read the famously smutty comic book Viz, which has several Geordie characters.

WHY 'GEORDIE' & 'MAKEM'?

No one is sure why the inhabitants of Newcastle upon Tyne are called **Geordies**. Some say it's a reference to 'Mad' King George III (**Geordie** is a diminutive of 'George') and by extension any unpredictable or undesirable person.

An inhabitant of Sunderland, the city just across the River Tyne from Newcastle, is called a **Makem** (the first syllable rhymes with 'pack'). The word is said to originate from a reference to the shipbuilding industry – once a major Tyneside employer: 'We make them and take them' (ie, we make them in the shipyard then take them down the river) which would be pronounced **we mak em and tak em**.

VOCABULARY

One of the features of the Geordie dialect is adding the word *like* to the end of sentences, usually for emphasis: *He's a canny snooker player like*.

There are many other oddities, but the following will give you some basics:

aye	yes (hence the classic Geordie phrase *way aye* – 'why yes', meaning 'absolutely')
bairn	child; baby
canny	clever; good; crafty; enjoyable (an all-purpose term of approval – a particular pub in Northumberland displays this sign: *Canny Ale, Canny Food, Canny Crack*)
champion	great, terrific
chin	break (*Sorry mam, I chinned a plate*)
clarts	mud (*Me clobber's aal clarty* – 'My clothes are all dirty')
divvent	don't, doesn't (*Divvent dee that!* meaning 'Don't do that!')
gadgie	an old man, or sometimes an old woman
gan	go (*Let's gan to the pub*)
geet	very (*Wor lass is geet bonny* – 'My wife's very pretty')
glair/glaur	mud
glaky	slow-witted
hadaway	go away; also an expression of disbelief
hinny	term of endearment, like 'honey'
howay/haway	away; let's go; also an expression of disbelief (*Howay man, ah divvent believe that like!*)
hoy	to throw (*Hoy it oot the winda!* – 'Throw it out of the window!')
hyem	home
lass	girl or young woman; *wor lass* (my lass) means 'my wife'
man	term of address for use with men, women and even small children: *Put aal your toys away Darren man*

marrer	(work)mate
mortal	drunk
nettie	toilet
pallatic	drunk (from 'paralytic')
pickle	a small quantity (*Gi'us a pickle mair* – 'Give me a bit more')
poke	bag
scutty	scruffy

WHAT'S THE CRACK?

In the northeast, the word *crack* has a varied job description. For example, *What's the crack?* means 'What's happening?' but *good crack* means 'a good time'. An answer to 'Why are you doing it?' could be *For the crack* (ie 'for the fun'). The word can also mean simply 'talk', 'chat' or 'gossip'.

The word *crack* is widely used in other parts of Britain and in Ireland (where it's spelt 'craic').

Wales

Wales is a separate country (called a *principality*) within Britain that came under the control of the English king Edward I in the 12th century, and was formally united with England in 1535. Despite several centuries of enforced anglicisation, Welsh – a Celtic language, totally different to English – has managed to survive, and since the 1980s has been enjoying a renaissance. (More details on the Welsh language are given in the next chapter.)

Many Welsh people – particularly in the north and west of the country – speak Welsh as a first language and English as a second language. In the south, English is generally the first language, but most people speak or understand some Welsh, and Welsh is a compulsory subject in schools. Consequently, the English spoken in Wales is heavily influenced by the Welsh accent and vocabulary.

Wales

Percentage of population over 3 years old speaking **Welsh**

- 60–70%
- 50–60%
- 40–50%
- 20–30%
- 10–20%
- 2–10%

GREAT BRITAIN

ACCENT

Features of the Welsh accent when speaking English include the frequent dropping of the *h* sound and a tendency to pronounce *f* more like a *v*, so that the English city of Hereford (just over the border from Wales) would be pronounced *Erevod* (pronounced as three syllables: 'e-re-vod'). You may also hear Welsh people 'doubling' the consonants in English words. The word 'patter' for example comes out more like 'pat-ter'. The same thing happens with words like 'cottage', 'adding', 'rubber' or 'village'.

Another very noticeable feature of Welsh English is its 'sing-song' intonation, which has been carried over from the Welsh language.

VOCABULARY

Some of the vocabulary used in Wales, and the way it's used, also owes its origin to the Welsh language. For example, a Welsh speaker might say *Look at that trousers* – because the word for 'trousers' is singular in Welsh. Another common feature in Welsh English is the use of *there's* – Welsh people may say *There's lovely!* or *There's cosy!* instead of 'That's lovely!' or 'How cosy!'

Listen out too for the unique Welsh use of the word *now*, as in *I'll be there now* (from the Welsh phrase *Bydda i 'na nawr*, pronounced 'beetha i na nawr'). 'Now' doesn't always mean 'this very moment'; it can also mean 'a short time in the future', so *I'll be there now* means 'I'll be there in a few minutes'. Similarly, Welsh people speaking English use the word *to* in a way speakers of standard English may find unusual. For example *Where's my wallet to?* means 'Where's my wallet?' Hence the following mobile phone conversation:

John: *We're in the pub already. Where're you to?*
Jim: *I'm just getting off the bus. I'll be there now.*

The English spoken in Wales also makes great use of the handy catch-all phrase *is it?* at the end of a sentence, regardless of the verb that went before it. So you might hear, for example, *Wales are playing England at rugby tomorrow, is it?* as opposed to 'Wales are playing England at rugby tomorrow, are they?' *Is it?* is most commonly used, however, as an all-purpose response meaning something like 'Oh, right', or 'Did you?' as in:

Jack: *We went to Newport yesterday.*
Dai: *Is it?*

Below is a list of words commonly used in Welsh English. Many are Welsh words simply carried over from the Welsh language to English, either in their original form or with some anglicisation along the way:

bach	(pronounced like 'Bach' the composer, but with the *a* as in 'bag'; from the Welsh for 'small') child; a term of friendship or endearment (*All right, bach?* is the equivalent of 'All right, mate?')
bad	ill, unwell (also used in many other dialects in England)
bailey	backyard; the gap between the front door and the gate of a house
butty	friend (possibly the origin of the US term 'buddy')
cammit	crooked (from Welsh *cam* meaning 'crooked')
cwm	valley (pronounced 'coom', but with the vowel not as long as in English 'coombe')
lairy	weary
lonk	hungry

lose	miss (*He lost the bus*)
mitch	play truant
off	hostile, angry
petty	toilet
pilm	dust
pursy/putsy	easy
simple	ill, unwell
sorty	proud
tidy	can mean 'good-looking' (as in *she's a tidy girl*), 'well done' (*a tidy job*), 'properly' (as in *Sing it again, but this time do it tidy*) or 'decent' (*he's a tidy sort of bloke*)
top room	sitting room, best room, parlour
trwstan	clumsy (pronounced 'troostan')
tump	hill, mound (from Welsh *twmp* meaning 'hill')
twp	simple, slow-witted (pronounced 'toop' – see pronunciation of *cwm*)

As well as borrowing Welsh words and/or usage, Welsh English has a tendency to follow Welsh grammar, meaning word order is sometimes changed to emphasise a particular aspect of the sentence. So *Hurt she was* brings the injury into sharper focus, and *Terrible they played* or *Awful I thought it sounded* give the 'terribleness' and 'awfulness' centre stage.

A SMALL PROBLEM

The Welsh enjoy telling the (apocryphal) story of English incomers who move to Wales and decide to give their cottage a new name. Referring to the Welsh–English dictionary, they come up with *Ty Bach*, meaning 'small house' – not realising that this is also the Welsh for 'toilet'.

Scotland

Forming the northern part of Britain, Scotland is another separate country within the United Kingdom. Devolution (partial autonomy) came to Scotland in 1999 with the opening of the nation's own parliament in Edinburgh, after 300 years of rule from London. Even before this, Scotland stood apart from England by maintaining its own legal system, educational system, cultural traditions, and – of course – languages.

In the same way that the Welsh language influenced the English spoken in Wales, so the English dialects spoken in Scotland have been influenced by its two indigenous languages – **Scottish Gaelic** (pronounced *gah*·lik), often known as **Highland Scots**, and **Lallans** or **Lowland Scots**. The names reflect the areas where they are or were spoken – the Highlands is essentially the north and west of Scotland. They also give the erroneous impression that Highland Scots and Lowland Scots are two variants of the same language, when they are in fact completely unrelated. Scottish Gaelic is a Celtic tongue related to Welsh; Lallans is a Germanic language closely related to English, with influences from Old Norse (more details in the following chapter).

As with all the other regions described in this book, there's a wide range of dialects in Scotland – the words and accents you'll hear in Inverness, for example, are very different from those in Glasgow. In the areas where English has been spoken for a long time – the Borders region in the south of Scotland, the east coast between Perth and Aberdeen, and the so-called Central Belt containing Glasgow and Edinburgh and

Scotland

Orkney Islands
Duncansby Head

NORTH SEA

Lewis
Stornoway
Harris
The Minch
North Uist
Little Minch
Benbecula
South Uist
Skye
Barra
Sea of the Hebrides
Rum
Eigg
Coll
Tiree
Mull

Dornoch Firth
Moray Firth
Elgin
Fraserburgh

Inverness
Loch Ness

Ben Nevis
▲ (1344m)

Grampians
Aberdeen
Stonehaven

ATLANTIC OCEAN

Colonsay
Jura

Islay

Oban
SCOTLAND

Loch Lomond
Stirling
Dumbarton
Greenock
Glasgow
Bute
Motherwell
Kilmarnock

Perth
Dundee
St Andrews Bay

Kirkcaldy
Firth of Forth

Edinburgh

Lammermuir Hills

0   50 km
0   30 mi

Campbeltown
Kintyre

Arran

Ayr

Southern Uplands

Hawick

ENGLAND

Pennines

NORTHERN IRELAND

North Channel

Stranraer
Machars

Dumfries

Solway Firth

Belfast ⊕

Percentage of population over 3 years
old speaking **Scottish Gaelic**

■ 70–75%	■ 20–30%
■ 60–70%	■ 10–20%
■ 50–60%	■ 2–10%
■ 40–50%	■ 0%
■ 30–40%	

GREAT BRITAIN

Scotland

197

the surrounding areas – distinct versions of English have developed which can be difficult for outsiders to penetrate.

In contrast, in the Highlands and in Scotland's numerous islands the widespread use of English is a relatively recent development, and so the English spoken in these areas does not contain many dialect terms.

ACCENT

One of the most obvious features of the Scottish accent is the use of the trilled *r* in words like 'car', 'four', 'barn' and 'first' (used in an emphasised form by cartoon characters Scrooge McDuck and Willy the janitor from *The Simpsons*). You'll also hear the guttural *ch* sound (as in 'Bach') used quite a bit by Scots, in words like *loch* or the exclamation *Och!*

Also, in Scottish English the vowel sounds in many words are different: the word 'home' is pronounced *hame*, 'stone' is *stane*, 'long' is *lang*, 'head' is *heed* and 'dead' is pronounced *deed*. 'House' is *hoose*, 'down' is *doon* and 'out' is *oot*.

VOCABULARY

Some grammatical constructions you may hear in Scottish English may appear unusual. For example:

My hair needs washed.
  My hair needs washing.

I might could go tomorrow.
  I might be able to go tomorrow.

There it's!
  There it is!

That cup is mines.
  That cup is mine.

(The last example might sound odd, but if you think about it, it's more logical than Standard English where 'his', 'hers', 'yours' 'ours' 'theirs' all have an *s* on the end, but 'mine' for some reason doesn't.)

Other constructions include the use of *will I* where 'shall I' would be used in Standard English (eg *Will I put this bread in a bag for you?*) and *that's me* meaning 'I'm finished'. *I'm away* means 'I'm leaving now'. *Outwith* means 'outside'.

For the word 'today' some Scots tend to say *the day* (which is, incidentally, the derivation of the word in standard English) and for 'tomorrow', *the morn*. *The morn's morn* is 'tomorrow morning'.

Scottish English also makes a distinction between the singular and plural forms of 'you'. The singular is the recognisable *you*; the plural is *youse* (pronounced 'yooz') – eg *Are youse kids coming doon?* (Several other dialects of English, in Britain and beyond, also make this distinction.)

Of the urban dialects, those from Glasgow and Edinburgh are perhaps the best known. The pronunciation and intonation differences between them are fairly minor – have a listen to Glaswegian comedian Billy Connolly and you'll get the gist. For a sample of the English spoken in Edinburgh watch the classic movie *Trainspotting*.

There's only enough space here to list a tiny proportion of Scottish dialect terms, but below is a taster of some of the words and phrases you may come across. Some words are Gaelic or Lallans in origin, either used in their original form in Scottish English, or with anglicised spelling.

ay	(pronounced 'eye') yes
aye	(pronounced 'eye') always – so a letter may be signed *Aye yours, Fiona*
barry	excellent, as in *That match was pure barry*
ben	hill or mountain (from Gaelic *beinn*)
blether	blather, drivel, waffle
bogging	disgusting; unpleasant; ugly (pronounced 'boggin')
bowfing	disgusting; unpleasant; ugly (pronounced 'bowfin')

braw	great, good
burn	stream, brook
cannae	cannot
cauld	cold
ceilidh	party, dance, get-together (Gaelic for 'gathering', pronounced 'kaylee')
cheg	steal
clan	family; group of related families (from Gaelic *clann*, meaning 'children')
clanjamfrie/ clamjamfry	a crowd; odds and ends
clarty	dirty; muddy
clinging	disgusting; unpleasant; ugly (pronounced 'clingin')
clipe	to tell on someone
crabbit	bad-tempered, sullen
dinnae	do not
dram	a measure of spirits (eg *Will you stop by for a dram of whisky?*)
dreich	miserable, wet, gloomy (of weather)
forbye	as well, also
gallus	mischievous
gey	very (*It's gey cauld today*)
glaikit	slow-witted
glen	valley (from Gaelic *gleann*)
gnash	hurry (*C'mon youse, gnash!*)
gowk	idiot, fool (literally 'cuckoo')
greet	cry (*Dinnae greet, it's only a skelf!* – 'Don't cry, it's only a splinter!')
haar	thick, damp mist coming in off the sea
Haud yer whisht!	Be quiet!
haver	to chatter aimlessly or foolishly, to waffle
hen	term of endearment (toward women); when used by men discussing women, it means 'babe' or 'chick' (eg *Andrew, you said we'd meet a couple of hens tonight*)
Jings!	an exclamation along the lines of 'Good heavens!'

WHAT'S IN A NAME?

In former times Scots had its own semi-standardised spelling system, which included some unusual conventions. For example, *z* was pronounced *ng* or *y*, so Scots names like *Menzies* and *Dalziel* should be pronounced 'mingis' and 'dayell'. Likewise, the *quh* in *Urquhart*, *Farquhar*, *Colquhoun* and *Balquhidder* was not a *kw* sound, but a puff of air, like the sound you make when blowing out a candle. So *Colquhoun* is 'colhoon' and *Balquhidder* (where you can see Rob Roy's grave) is 'balwhidder'. *Urquhart* and *Farquhar*, however, have given up the fight and are now generally pronounced 'urkart' and 'farkwar'.

ken	know
loch	lake
loup	to run; to jump
lum	chimney
minging	disgusting; unpleasant; ugly (pronounced 'mingin')
muckle/mickle	big
nip	a measure of spirits (smaller than a *dram*)
nyaff	idiot
outwith	without
pech	pant, puff (often after climbing a *ben*)
radge	slightly deranged person (*Ignore him, he's a radge*); exciting or out of the ordinary (*He's totally radge, that guy*)
rare	great, good
reek	smoke (hence *Auld Reekie* 'Old Smoky', the nickname for Edinburgh)
Sassenach	slightly insulting term for an English person (from the Gaelic word for 'Saxon'), although sometimes applied to any non-Highlander or non-Gaelic-speaking Scot
scaff	tramp; badly dressed person
scunnered	disgusted, repelled
shan	bad; awful; unkind

shoogle	shake
Slàinte!	Cheers! (pronounced 'sland-ge')
stoor	dust
stoorie	hurry; run away
strath	valley (from Gaelic *srath*)
swally	(alcoholic) drink
Teuchter	a Highlander (mocking)
wouldnae	would not
yon	that, like old English term 'yonder' (eg *Do you ken yon laddie?* – 'Do you know that boy over there?')

IMPENETRABLE AS GRANITE

Any language difficulties you may have in Glasgow or Edinburgh are nothing compared to those associated with the Aberdeen dialect. The Scandinavian influence is stronger in Aberdeen (nicknamed the Granite City) than anywhere else in Scotland, as boats from Norway and Denmark call in here, and it's sometimes hard to tell apart the speech of these tourists and that of the Aberdonian locals using their broadest vernacular. A common greeting is *Fit like?* ('How are you?'), which can be answered *Tyaavin awa* meaning 'I'm fine' or *Gweed* ('Good'). If a tourist is asked *Far d'ye bide?* ('Where do you live?') and the answer's Australia, a local might say *Ah hine awa* ('Ah, far away'). A few other local words are *foggie-bummers* (bumblebees) and *horny-gollochs* (earwigs). Foreigners are *fremmit* and *dubs* is mud.

Welsh

Although Welsh people speak English, a few words of Welsh (*Cymraeg* kuhm·*raig*) will be appreciated by locals. Welsh is the strongest of the Celtic languages, both in terms of number of speakers (over 500,000) and its place in society. The language belongs to the Celtic branch of the Indo-European family – it's closely related to Breton and Cornish, and more distantly to Irish, Scottish and Manx. At one time it was spoken throughout the island of Britain south of a line between modern Glasgow and Edinburgh, but was gradually pushed westwards by the invading Angles and Saxons in the 5th century.

Up until the Industrial Revolution most Welsh people spoke only Welsh, but by the early modern period Welsh had lost its status as an official language. In 1900 some 50 per cent still spoke Welsh; by 1961, however, only 26 per cent were Welsh-speaking and there was general alarm that the language would disappear.

The following year Saunders Lewis's BBC radio lecture *Tynged yr Iaith* tuhng·ed uhr yaith (The Fate of the Language) led to the creation of *Cymdeithas yr Iaith Gymraeg* kuhm·*day*·thas uhr yaith guhm·*raig* (The Welsh Language Society), a protest movement in support of the language. Its civil disobedience campaigns succeeded in

AT A GLANCE ...

Language name: Welsh

Name in language:
Cymraeg kuhm·*raig*

Language family: Celtic

Key country: Wales

Approximate number of speakers: 500,000 plus

Close relatives: Breton, Cornish, Irish, Scottish Gaelic

Donations to English: bard, booth, car, combe, coracle, corgi, crumpet, dad, flannel

Welsh

203

winning equal recognition for Welsh in one domain of society after another. Recent figures suggest that the decline has been halted, and Welsh has enjoyed a resurgence as a badge of national identity.

PRONUNCIATION

Stress in Welsh almost always falls on the penultimate syllable of a word. In the pronunciation guides, words are divided into syllables by a dot and stressed syllables are italicised.

Vowel sounds

Symbol	English equivalent	Welsh example	Transliteration
a	act	*cam*	kam
ah	father	*da*	dah
ai	aisle	*saith*	saith
ay	hay	*peint*	paynt
e	pen	*het*	het
ee	see	*dyn*	deen
eh	there	*hen*	hehn
ew	few	*duw*	dew
i	sin	*cyn*	kin
o	hot	*ffon*	fon
oh	oh	*sôn*	sohn
oo	fool	*mwg*	moog
ow	now	*naw*	now
oy	boy	*coes*	koys
u	put	*cwm*	kum
uh	ago	*yn*	uhn

Consonant sounds

Symbol	English equivalent	Welsh example	Transliteration
b	**box**	*b*ryd	breed
d	**dog**	*d*yn	deen
dh	**th**is	*dd*oe	dhoy
f	**fun**	*ff*ordd	fohrdh
g	**game**	*g*lan	glan
h	**hat**	*h*af	hahv
hl	**h and l together with a puff of air**	*ll*yn	hlin
hr	**h and r together with a puff of air**	*rh*iw	hrew
j	**jump**	*j*am	jam
k	**cat**	*c*i	kee
kh	**loch**	ba*ch*	bakh
l	**laugh**	*l*awnt	lownt
m	**meal**	*m*awr	mowr
n	**naughty**	*n*os	nohs
ng	si**ng**	a*ng*en	*ang*·en
p	**price**	*p*en	pen
r	**red (trilled)**	*c*arw	ka·roo
s	**sin**	*s*ant	sant
sh	**shell**	*s*iop	shop
t	**tickle**	*t*iwn	teewn
th	**thick**	ca*th*	kath
v	**vat**	*f*yny	*vuh*·nee
w	**wee**	*chw*erw	khwe·roo
y	**yes**	*i*awn	yown

NUMBERS

0	*dim*	dim
1	*un*	een
2	*dau/dwy* m/f	dai/*doo*·ee
3	*tri/tair* m/f	tree/tair
4	*pedwar/pedair* m/f	ped·wahr/*pe*·dair
5	*pump*	pimp
6	*chwech*	khwehkh
7	*saith*	saith
8	*wyth*	oo·ith
9	*naw*	now
10	*deg*	dehg

TIME & DATES

Days

Monday	*Dydd Llun* m	deedh hleen
Tuesday	*Dydd Mawrth* m	deedh mowrth
Wednesday	*Dydd Mercher* m	deedh *mehr*·kher
Thursday	*Dydd Iau* m	deedh yai
Friday	*Dydd Gwener* m	deedh *gwe*·ner
Saturday	*Dydd Sadwrn* m	deedh *sa*·doorn
Sunday	*Dydd Sul* m	deedh seel

HAPPY DAYS

Happy Birthday!
Pen-Blwydd Hapus! pen·*bloo*·idh *ha*·pis

Happy Christmas!
Nadolig Llawen! na·*do*·lig *hlow*·en

Happy New Year!
Blwyddyn Newydd Da! *bloo*·idh·in *neh*·widh dhah

Months

Half of the names of the months in Welsh were originally borrowed from Latin, and half (those that have literal translations below) are Welsh.

January	*Mis Ionawr* m	mees *yoh*·nowr
February	*Mis Chwefror* m	mees *khwev*·ror
March	*Mis Mawrth* m	mees mowrth
April	*Mis Ebrill* m	mees *eb*·rihl
May	*Mis Mai* m	mees mai
June	*Mis Mehefin* m	mees me·*he*·vin
	(lit: middle-of-summer)	
July	*Mis Gorffennaf* m	mees gor·*fe*·nav
	(lit: end-of-summer)	
August	*Mis Awst* m	mees owst
September	*Mis Medi* m	mees *me*·di
	(lit: reaping)	
October	*Mis Hydref* m	mees *huhd*·rev
	(lit: stag-roaring, ie rutting season)	
November	*Mis Tachwedd* m	mees *takh*·wedh
	(lit: slaughter)	
December	*Mis Rhagfyr* m	mees *hrag*·veer
	(lit: before-short, ie before the shortest day)	

Seasons

spring	*Gwanwyn* m	*gwan*·win
summer	*Haf* m	hahv
autumn	*Hydref* m	*huhd*·rev
winter	*Gaeaf* m	*gay*·av

Time

minute	*munud* f	*mi*·nid
hour	*awr* f	owr
week	*wythnos* f	oo·*ith*·nos
	(lit: eight-nights)	
month	*mis* m	mees
today	*heddiw*	*hedh*·yoo
tomorrow	*yfory*	uh·*voh*·ree

LANGUAGE DIFFICULTIES

I speak a little Welsh.
Dw i'n siarad tipyn   doo een *sha*·rad *ti*·pin
bach o Gymraeg.   bakh o guhm·*raig*

I don't understand.
Dw i ddim yn deall.   doo ee dhim uhn *day*·ahl

Could you speak more slowly, please?
Allwch chi siarad yn   *a*·hlookh khee *sha*·rad uhn
arafach, os gwelwch   *a·ra·*vakh os *gwe·*lookh
yn dda?   uhn dhah

Could you repeat that?
Allwch chi ddweud   *a*·hlookh khee dhwaid
hynny eto?   *huh*·nee *e*·to

Could you write that down, please?
Allwch chi sgrifennu   *a*·hlookh khee sgri·*ve*·nee
hynny i lawr, os   *huh*·nee ee lowr os
gwelwch yn dda?   *gwe·*lookh uhn dhah

How do you say …?
Sut mae dweud …?   sit mai dwaid …

What's this called in Welsh?
Beth yw hwn yn Gymraeg?   beth ew hun uhn guhm·*raig*

MEETING PEOPLE

Greetings, goodbyes & civilities

Hello.
Sut mae.   sit mai

Good morning.
Bore da.   *boh*·re dah

Good afternoon.
Prynhawn da.   *prin*·hown dah

Good evening.
Noswaith dda.   *nos*·waith dhah

Goodnight.
Nos da.   nohs dah

See you (later).
Wela i chi (wedyn). we·la ee khee (*we*·din)

How are you?
Sut ydych chi? sit *uh*·dikh khee

(Very) well.
Da (iawn). dah (yown)

Goodbye.
Hwyl fawr. hoo·il vowr

Excuse me.
Esgusodwch fi. es·gi·so·dookh vee

May I?
Ga i? gah ee

Do you mind?
Oes ots gyda chi? oys ots *gi*·da khee

Sorry.
Mae'n ddrwg gen i. main dhroog gen ee

Please.
Os gwelwch yn dda. os *gwe*·lookh uhn dhah

Thank you (very much).
Diolch (yn fawr iawn). dyolkh (uhn vowr yown)

You're welcome.
Croeso. kroy·so

Don't mention it.
Peidiwch â sôn. pay·dyookh a sohn

I don't know.
Wn i ddim. oon ee dhim

Yes/No.
Ie/Nage. yeh/*nah*·geh

We have given words for 'yes' and 'no' above, but these are only used in certain circumstances – in general, you respond to a question in Welsh with a positive or negative form of the question's verb. For example, 'Are you going to Swansea?' would be answered either 'I am' or 'I'm not'.

Making conversation

What's your name?
Beth yw eich enw chi?   beth ew aykh e·noo khee

My name's …
Fy enw i yw …   vuh e·noo ee ew …

I'd like to introduce you to …
Ga i gyflwyno … i chi.   gah ee guh·vloo·i·no … ee khee

Pleased to meet you.
Mae'n dda gen i gwrdd   main dhah gen i goordh
â chi.   a khee

Where do you live?
Ble ydych chi'n byw?   bleh uh·dikh kheen bee·oo

I live in (Darwin).
Dw i'n byw yn (Darwin).   doo een bee·oo uhn (dahr·win)

I'm here …	*Dw i yma …*	doo ee uh·ma …
on business	*ar fusnes*	ahr vis·nes
on holiday	*ar wyliau*	ahr wil·yai
studying	*yn astudio*	uhn as·tid·yo

WELL-WISHING

Cheers!
Iechyd Da!   ye·khid dah

Get well soon!
Brysiwch wella!   bruh·shookh we·hla

Bless you! (for sneezing)
Bendith!   ben·dith

What a pity!
Dyna drueni!   duh·na dree·eh·ni

Bon voyage!
Siwrnai dda!   shoor·ne dhah

Good luck!
Pob lwc!   pob luk

Hope it goes well!
Pob hwyl!   pob hoo·il

BACKGROUND

Where are you from?	O ble ydych chi'n dod?	o bleh *uh*·dikh kheen dohd
I'm from …	Dw i'n dod o …	doo een dohd o …
Australia	Awstralia	ow·*stra*·lya
Canada	Ganada	*ga*·na·da
England	Loegr	*loy*·guhr
Ireland	Iwerddon	i·*wehr*·dhon
New Zealand	Seland Newydd	*say*·land *neh*·widh
Scotland	Yr Alban	uhr *al*·ban
the USA	Yr Unol Daleithiau	uhr *ee*·nol da·*lay*·thee·ai
What do you do?	Beth ydych chi'n wneud?	beth *uh*·dikh kheen w·*naid*
I'm a/an …	Dw i'n …	doo een …
artist	arlunydd m&f	ar·*li*·nidh
business-person	berson m&f busnes m&f	*ber*·son *bis*·nes
doctor	feddyg m&f	*ve*·dhig
engineer	beiriannydd m&f	bay·ree·*a*·nidh
journalist	newyddi-adurwr m newyddi-adurwraig f	ne·*wuh*·dhee·a·*dee*·roor ne·*wuh*·dhee·a·*dee*·raig
lawyer	gyfreithwraig f gyfreithiwr m	giv·*rayth*·raig giv·*rayth*·yoor
musician	gerddor m&f	*ger*·dhor
nurse	nyrs m&f	nuhrs
secretary	ysgrifennydd m ysgrife-nyddes f	uhs·gri·*ve*·nidh uhs·gri·ve·*nuh*·dhes
teacher	athro m athrawes f	*ath*·ro *ath*·*row*·es
waiter	weinydd	*way*·nidh
waitress	weinyddes	way·*nudh*·es

I work in an office.	Dw i'n gweithio mewn swyddfa.	doo een *gwayth*·yo *meh*·oon *sweedh*·va
I'm ...	Dw i ...	doo ee ...
retired	wedi ymddeol	*we*·dee uhm·*dhay*·ol
unemployed	yn ddi-waith	uhn *dhee*·waith

INTERESTS

What do you like doing?
Beth ydych chi'n hoffi wneud?
beth *uh*·dikh kheen *ho*·fee w·*naid*

I like (swimming) and (going to the cinema).
Dw i'n hoffi (nofio) a (mynd i'r sinema).
doo een *ho*·fee (*nov*·yo) a (mind eer *si*·ne·ma)

I don't like (cooking).
Dw i ddim yn hoffi (coginio).
doo ee dhim uhn *ho*·fee (ko·*gin*·yo)

What do you do in your spare time?
Beth ydych chi'n wneud yn eich amser hamdden?
beth *uh*·dikh kheen w·*naid* uhn aykh *am*·ser *ham*·dhen

I play (chess).
Dw i'n chwarae (gwyddbwyll).
doo een khwah·*ray* (*gwidh*·bwihl)

Do you like (sport)?
Ydych chi'n hoffi (chwaraeon)?
uh·dikh kheen *ho*·fee (khwah·*ray*·on)

Yes, very much.
Ydw, yn fawr iawn.
uh·*doo* uhn vowr yown

No, not at all.
Nac ydw, dim o gwbl.
nak uh·*doo* dim o *gu*·bul

ARTY WORDS

Welsh has a long and illustrious musical and literary history, beginning in the 6th century with court poets Taliesin and Aneurin, in what is now southern Scotland, and continuing to the present day.

cerdd dant   kehrdh dant
Strict-metre poetry sung in counterpoint to a tune on the harp.

cynghanedd   kuhng·*ha*·nedh
A system of consonance or alliteration in a line of strict-metre Welsh poetry.

eisteddfod   ay·*stedh*·vod
A competitive arts festival.

GOING OUT

What are you doing this evening?
Beth ydych chi'n   beth *uh*·dikh kheen
wneud heno?   w·*naid* he·no

Nothing special.
Dim byd arbennig.   dim beed ar·*be*·nig

Would you like to go out somewhere?
Hoffech chi fynd   *ho*·fekh khee vind
allan i rywle?   *a*·hlan ee *rew*·le

Would you like to go for a drink/meal?
Hoffech chi fynd allan am   *ho*·fekh khee vind *a*·hlan am
ddiod/bryd o fwyd?   *dhee*·od/breed o *voo*·id

I'll buy.
Fe dala i.   veh *da*·la ee

Do you feel like (going for a swim)?
Oes awydd (mynd i   oys *ow*·idh (mind ee
nofio) arnoch chi?   *nov*·yo) ar·nokh khee

Yes, that'd be lovely.
Hoffwn, byddai   *ho*·foon *buh*·dhai
hynny'n hyfryd.   *huh*·neen *huh*·vrid

Yes, where to?
Hoffwn. Ble awn ni?   ho·foon bleh own nee

Yes, that'd be great.
Oes, byddai hynny'n wych.   oys buh·dhai huh·neen weekh

OK.
Iawn.   yown

No, I'm afraid I can't.
Alla i ddim, mae   a·hla ee dhim mai
arna i ofn.   ar·na ee o·vuhn

I'm sorry, I can't.
Mae'n ddrwg gen i,   main dhroog gen ee
alla i ddim.   a·hla ee dhim

Not at the moment, thanks.
Ddim ar hyn o   dhim ahr hin o
bryd, diolch.   breed dyolkh

What about tomorrow?
Beth am yfory?   beth am uh·voh·ree

I feel like going to …
Mae gen i awydd   mai gen ee ow·idh
mynd i …   mind ee …

ARRANGING TO MEET

What time shall we meet?
Am faint o'r gloch   am vaint ohr glohkh
wnawn ni gyfarfod?   w·nown nee guh·var·vod

Where shall we meet?
Ble wnawn ni   bleh w·nown nee
gyfarfod?   guh·var·vod

Let's meet at (eight o'clock) in St Mary Street.
Beth am gyfarfod am   beth am guh·var·vod am
(wyth o'r gloch) yn   (oo·ith ohr glohkh) uhn
Heol y Santes Fair.   hay·ol uh san·tes vair

OK. I'll see you then.
Iawn. Wela i chi   yown wel·a ee khee
bryd hynny.   breed huh·nee

AFTERWARDS

It was nice talking to you.
    Roedd hi'n braf   roydh uhn brahv
    siarad â chi.   *sha*·rad a khee

I have to get going now.
    Rhaid imi fynd nawr.   hraid *ee*·mee vind nowr

I had a great day/evening.
    Ces i ddiwrnod   kehs ee *dyoor*·nod
    gwych/noson wych.   gweekh/*nos*·on weekh

Hope to see you again soon.
    Gobeithio eich gweld   go·*bayth*·yo aykh gweld
    chi eto yn fuan.   khee *et*·ohn *vee*·an

I'll give you a call.
    Ffônia i chi.   *fohn*·ya ee khee

What's your number?
    Beth yw eich rhif?   beth ew aykh hreev

WELSH PLACE NAMES

The town of Llanfairpwllgwyngyllgogerychwyrndrobwllllantysiliogogogoch (hlan·vair·poohl·*gwin*·gihl·go·gehr·uh·*khwuh* rn·dro·buhl·hlan·tuh·*sil*·yo·go·go·*gokh*) has legendary status as the longest place name in the UK. It translates as 'Saint Mary's Church in the hollow of the white hazel near a rapid whirlpool and the Church of St Tysilio of the red cave.' Here are some more humdrum Welsh town names and their translations:

Abertawe	*a*·ber·*tow*·eh	Swansea
Caergybi	kair·*guh*·bi	Holyhead
Casnewydd	kas·*neh*·widh	Newport

FOOD & DRINK

Eating Out

A table for ..., please.
Bwrdd i ... os gwelwch   boordh ee ... os *gwe*·lookh
yn dda.   uhn dhah

Can I see the menu, please?
Ga i weld y fwydlen,   gah ee weld uh *voo*·eed·len
os gwelwch yn dda?   os *gwe*·lookh uhn dhah

The bill, please.
Y bil, os gwelwch yn dda.   uh bil os *gwe*·lookh uhn dhah

In the Pub

I'd like a (half)	Ga i (hanner o)	gah ee (*han*·er oh)
pint of ...	beint o ...	baynt oh ...
bitter	chwerw	*khwe*·roo
cider	seidr	*say*·duhr
lager	lager	*lah*·guhr

TRADITIONAL DISHES

bara brith m   *ba*·ra breeth
  A rich, fruit tea-loaf.

bara lawr m   *ba*·ra lowr
  Laver seaweed boiled and mixed with oatmeal and
  traditionally served with bacon for breakfast.

cawl m   kowl
  A broth of meat and vegetables.

caws caerffili m   kows kair·*fi*·li
  Caerphilly cheese, a crumbly salty cheese that used to
  be popular with miners.

ffagots a phys f   *fa*·gots a fees
  Balls of chopped pork and liver in gravy served with peas.

pice f **ar y maen** m   *pi*·ke ahr uh main
  Literally 'cakes on the griddlestone': small, scone-like
  fruit griddle cakes, also known as **Welsh cakes**.

Scottish Gaelic

As with the Welsh, all Scots speak English, but a little effort put into learning some phrases in Scottish Gaelic (*Gàidhlig gah·lik*) will be rewarded. Just keep in mind that of the roughly 60,000 people who speak Scottish Gaelic, most live in the Highlands and Islands in the west and northwest of Scotland. Increasing numbers also live in or near large urban centres such as Glasgow and Edinburgh. Outside the Highlands, though, you may get blank looks if you venture anything more complicated than a greeting in Gaelic!

Scottish Gaelic belongs to the Goidelic branch of Celtic. Irish (*Gaeilge*), and Manx (*Gaelg*), an extinct language from the Isle of Man, are closely related to Scottish Gaelic.

It's generally believed that Gaelic was brought to Scotland by Irish settlers some time in or before the 5th century AD. The Romans called these settlers *Scotti* (literally 'Irishmen'), which later gave rise to the country's name. By the 11th and 12th centuries, Scottish Gaelic was spoken in most parts of modern Scotland. However, from this point up to the late 19th century, Gaelic was in decline for much of the time, beginning in the Lowlands where there was most English influence and persecution. Gaelic flourished in the Highlands until the 18th century, the time of the Jacobite rebellions and wars. The dispersion forced by the Highland Clearances (*na Fuadaichean*, nuh foo·duh·khuhn) of the 19th century

---

AT A GLANCE ...

Language name:
Scottish Gaelic

Name in language:
Gàidhlig (na h-Alba)
*gah·*lik
(nuh *hah·*luh·puh)

Language family: Celtic

Key countries: Scotland, Canada

Approximate number of speakers: 60,000

Close relatives:
Irish Gaelic, Manx

Donations to English:
brogue, clan, glen, galore, jilt, loch, slogan, strontium, whisky

and the destruction of the Gaelic school system by the *1872 Education Act (Scotland)* did further damage.

Fortunately, the tide has since turned, due to efforts from the later 19th century to raise the profile of Gaelic and increase the confidence of speakers in their language and culture. A measure of security has also been granted by the UK's 2001 ratification of the European Charter for Regional or Minority Languages.

PRONUNCIATION

Stress in Scottish Gaelic almost always falls on the first syllable of a word. Stressed syllables are italicised in the pronunciation guides.

Vowel sounds

Note that the r is not pronounced in the er sound listed below.

Symbol	English equivalent	Gaelic example	Transliteration
ah	father	*tha*	hah
ai	aisle	*chaidh*	hai
aw	raw	*loch*	lawkh
e	hex	*bean*	ben
ee	see	*mi*	mee
eh	hair	*air*	ehr
er	her	*aon*	ern
i	sin	*fios*	fis
oh	oh	*mòr*	mohr
oo	hoot	*ugh*	oo
ow	cow	*ann*	own
oy	boy	*dòigh*	doy
uh	ago	*agam*	*ah*·kuhm

Consonant sounds

Symbol	English equivalent	Gaelic example	Transliteration
b	**b**ox	*bòrd*	borsht
ch	**ch**eese	*àite*	ah·**ch**uh
d	**d**og	*duine*	*d*er·nyuh
f	**f**un	*fios*	fis
g	**g**ame	*gorm*	*g*aw·ruhm
gh	between g and the 'ch' in 'loch'	*a dhà*	uh **gh**ah
h	**h**at	*tha*	hah
j	**j**ump	*dìreach*	*j*ee·ruhkh
k	**c**at	*cas*	kas
kh	lo**ch**	*ach*	ahkh
l	**l**augh	*litir*	*l*ee·chuhr
m	**m**eal	*math*	mah
n	**n**aughty	*glan*	glahn
ng	si**ng**	*long*	lawngk
p	**p**en	*pìos*	pees
r	like 'tt' in 'bu**tt**er' said fast	*ruadh*	roo·uhgh
s	**s**in	*solus*	soh·luhs
sh	**sh**ell	*sìos*	shee·uhs
t	**t**ickle	*taigh*	tai
v	**v**at	*à-bheil*	uh·*vel*
w	**w**in	*uill*	wel
y	**y**es	*coimhead*	kaw·yuht

NUMBERS

0	*neoini*	*nyaw*·nee
1	*a h-aon*	uh hern
2	*a dhà*	uh ghah
3	*a trì*	uh tree
4	*a ceithir*	uh *keh*·hir
5	*a cóig*	uh *coh*·ik
6	*a sia*	uh *shee*·uh
7	*a seachd*	uh shahkhk
8	*a hochd*	uh hawkhk
9	*a naoi*	uh *ner*·ee
10	*a deich*	uh jehkh

TIME & DATES

Time

minute	*mionaid* f	*mi*·nuhch
hour	*uair* f	oo·uhr
week	*seachdain* f	*shahkh*·kuhn
month	*mìos* m	*mee*·uhs
today	*(an latha) an-diugh*	(uhn lah) uhn·*joo*
tomorrow	*a-màireach*	uh·*mah*·ruhkh

Days

Monday	*Diluain* m	jee·*loo*·uhn
Tuesday	*Dimàirt* m	jee·mahrshch
Wednesday	*Diciadaoin* m	jee·*kee*·uh·tuhn
Thursday	*Diardaoin* m	jee·*der*·een
Friday	*Dihaoine* m	jee·*hoo*·nyuh
Saturday	*Disathairne* m	jee·*sah*·huhr·nuh

There are two words used for 'Sunday' listed below – the first tends to be used by Catholics and Episcopalians, the second by Presbyterians.

Sunday	*Didòmhnaich* m	jee·*daw*·nikh
Sunday	*Latha na Sàbaid* m	lah nuh *sah*·pich

The word *latha* 'day' is now also commonly spelled *là*. The pronunciation, lah, is the same in both cases.

Months

January	*am Faoileach*	uhm *fer*·ee·luhkh
February	*an Gearran*	uhn *gya*·ruhn
March	*am Màrt*	uhm mahrsht
April	*an Giblean*	uhn *gip*·luhn
May	*an Cèitean*	uhn *keh*·chuhn
June	*an t-Ògmhios*	uhn *tawk*·vee·uhs
July	*an t-Iuchar*	uhn *choo*·khuhr
August	*an Lùnastal*	uhn *loo*·nuh·stuhl
September	*an t-Sultain*	uhn *tool*·tin
October	*an Dàmhair*	uhn *dah*·vuhr
November	*an t-Samhain*	uhn *tow*·in
December	*an Dùbhlachd*	uhn *doo*·luhkhk

HAPPY DAYS

There are plenty of occasions to celebrate in Scotland and below are Gaelic words for the major festivals. New Year's Eve, or *Oidhche Challainn* (*ai*·khuh *khah*·lin, also known in English as Hogmanay), sees friends and relatives visiting each other after the New Year has been rung in and exchanging drinks. This is commonly referred to as 'first footing'.

Christmas	*Là Nollaig*	lah *naw*·lik
New Year's Day	*Là na Bliadhna Ùire*	lah nuh *blee*·uh·nuh oo·ruh
Hallowe'en	*Oidhche Shamhna*	*ai*·khuh *how*·nuh
May Day	*Là Bealltainn*	lah *byowl*·tin
Lammas Day	*Là Lùnastail*	lah *loo*·nuh·stuhl
First day of spring	*Là Fhèill Brighde*	lah el *bree*·juh
New Year's Day	*Là na Bliadhna Ùire*	lah nuh *blee*·uh·nuh oo·ruh
Easter	*a' Chàisg*	uh khahshk
St Andrew's Day	*Fèill Anndrais*	fel *own*·drish

Seasons

spring	*an t-Earrach* m	uhn *chah*·ruhkh
summer	*an Samhradh* m	uhn *sow*·ruhgh
autumn	*am Foghar* m	uhm *foh*·uhr
winter	*an Geamhradh* m	uhn *gyow*·ruhgh

LANGUAGE DIFFICULTIES

You'll see inf, meaning 'informal', and pol, meaning 'polite' next to some phrases: the polite version should be used with people you don't know very well or who are older than you.

I don't understand.
Chan eil mi a' tuigsinn. khahn yel mee uh *took*·shin

Could you say that again?
An canadh tu/sibh sin uhn *kah*·nuh too/shif shin
a-rithist? inf/pol uh *ree*·ishch

Could you speak more slowly, please?
Am bruidhneadh tu air uhm *broo*·ee·nyuh too ehr
do shocair mas e do duh *haw*·kir mah sheh duh
thoil e? inf hawl eh

Am bruidhneadh sibh uhm *broo*·ee·nyuh shif
air ur socair mas e ehr oor *saw*·kir mah sheh
ur toil e? pol oor tawl eh

What's this in Gaelic?
Dè tha seo anns a' jeh hah shaw owns uh
Ghàidhlig? *ghah*·lik

Do you speak Gaelic?
A' bheil Gàidhlig uh vel *gah*·lik
agad/agaibh? inf/pol *ah*·kuht/*ah*·kif

Yes, a little.
Tha, beagan. hah *be*·kuhn

Not much.
Chan eil mòran. khahn yel *moh*·ran

I'm learning.
Tha mi ag hah mee uh
ionnsachadh. *gyoh*·suhkh·uhgh

Note that there aren't any words in Gaelic directly equivalent to 'yes' and 'no' – instead, a positive or negative form of the verb in the question is used. For example, 'Did you visit Robert?' would be answered either 'Did visit' or 'Didn't visit'.

DIRECTIONS

Where's the …?	Càite a' bheil …?	kah·chuh vel …
I want to go to the …	Tha mi ag iarraidh a dhol do …	hah mee gee·uh·ree uh ghawl doh …
airport	am port-adhair	uhm *pawrsht·*ahr
bank	am banca	uhm *bahn·*kuh
church	an eaglais	uhn *ek·*lish
cinema	an taigh-dhealbh	uhn tai·*yah·*luhv
ferry	an t-aiseag	uhn *tah·*shuhk
hotel	an taigh-òsta	uhn tai·*aw·*stuh
pub	an taigh-seinnse	uhn tai·*shehn·*shuh
library	an leabharlann	uhn *lyoh·*uhr·lown
post office	oifis a' phuist	*aw·*fish uh fooshch
shop	a' bhùth	uh voo
shops	na bhùthan	nuh *voo·*uhn
station	an stèisean	uhn *steh·*shuhn
swimming pool	an t-amar snàimh	uhn *tah·*muhr snahv
toilet	an taigh-beag	uhn *tai·*bek
tourist information centre	ionad fiosrachaidh luchd turais	*in·*uht *fis·*ruh·khee lookhk *too·*rish
town centre	meadhan a' bhaile	*mee·*uhn uh *vah·*luh

SIGNS

am Poileas	uhm paw·lis	Police
Ceud Mìle	keht mee·luh	A Hundred
Fàilte	fahl·chuh	Thousand Welcomes
Fàilte gu ...	fahl·chuh goo ...	Welcome to ...
Fòn	fohn	Telephone
Sràid	strahch	Street
Taigh-beag	tai bek	Toilet
Fir	feer	Men
Mnathan	muh·nah·huhn	Women
Taigh-tasgaidh	tai·tah·skee	Museum

It's ...	Tha e ...	hah eh ...
here	*an seo*	uhn shaw
there	*an sin*	uhn shin
over there (near)	*thall an sin*	howl uhn shin
over there (far)	*thall an siud*	howl uhn shoot
up there	*shuas an sin*	hoo·uhs uhn shin
down there	*shìos an sin*	hee·uhs uhn shin
near	*faisg air*	fashk ehr
(the shop)	*(a' bhùth)*	(uh voo)
past	*seachad air*	shah·khuht ehr
(the bank)	*(a' bhanca)*	(uh vahn·kuh)

MEETING PEOPLE

Greetings, goodbyes & civilities

Scottish Gaelic has no word for 'hello'. Instead, people greet others by asking how they are and making comments on the weather. However, expressions based on English are becoming more common.

What's your name?
Dè an t-ainm a tha ort? inf   jen *tah*·nuhm uh hawrsht
Dè an t-ainm a tha oirbh? pol   jen *tah*·nuhm uh *haw*·ruhf

How are you?
Ciamar a tha thu/   *kim*·uhr uh hah oo/
sibh? inf/pol   shif

Well.
Tha gu math.   hah goo mah

Not bad.
Chan eil dona.   khahn yel *daw*·nuh

Good morning.
Madainn mhath.   *mah*·tin vah

Good afternoon/evening.
Feasgar math.   *fes*·kuhr mah

Good night.
Oidhche mhath.   *ai*·khuh vah

It's a lovely day.
Tha là brèagha ann.   hah lah *bree*·uh own

It's cold today.
Tha e fuar an-diugh.   hah eh *foo*·uhr uhn·*joo*

It's raining.
Tha an t-uisge ann.   hah uhn *toosh*·kuh own

It's snowing.
Tha sneachd ann.   hah snyakh own

It's misty.
Tha ceò ann.   hah kyoh own

Goodbye. (lit: blessing with you)
Beannachd leat. sg inf   *byah*·nuhkhk laht

Goodbye. (lit: blessing with you)
Beannachd leibh. pl & sg pol   *byah*·nuhkhk laiv

Goodbye. (lit: the same to you)
Mar sin leat/leibh. inf/pol   mahr shin laht/laiv

Who are you?
Có thusa?   koh *oo*·suh

I'm ...
Is mise ...   *smee*·shuh ...

Thank you.	*Tapadh leat.* sg inf	*tah·puh laht*
Thank you.	*Tapadh leibh.* pl & sg pol	*tah·puh laiv*
Thanks.	*Taing.*	*tah·eeng*
Many thanks.	*Mòran taing.*	*moh·ruhn tah·eeng*
Please.	*Mas e do thoil e.* sg inf	mash eh duh hawl eh
Please.	*Mas e ur toil e.* pl & sg pol	mash eh oor tawl eh
You're welcome.	*'S e do bheatha.* sg inf	sheh duh *veh·huh*
You're welcome.	*'S e ur beatha.* pl & sg pol	sheh oor *beh·huh*
Excuse me.	*Gabh mo leisgeul.* sg inf	gahv muh *lesh·kuhl*
Excuse me.	*Gabhaibh mo leisgeul.* pl & sg pol	*gah·viv muh lesh·kuhl*
I'm sorry.	*Tha mi duilich.*	hah mee *doo·likh*
Come along.	*Trobhad.*	*troh·uht*
Let's go.	*Thugainn.*	*hoo·kin*
Go on.	*Siubhad.*	*shoo·uht*
Yuck!	*A ghia!*	uh *yee·*uh
Goodness me!	*A thiarcais fhèin!*	uh *heer·kish hehn*
Pardon me.	*(Dè) b'àill leibh.*	(jeh) bahl laiv
I don't mind.	*Tha mi coma.*	hah mee *koh·muh*

Making conversation

What do you like doing?
Dé as toil leat/leibh a bhith a' dèanamh? inf/pol — jehs tawl laht/laiv uh vee uh *dee·*uh·nuhv

Do you like …?
An toil leat/leibh …? inf/pol — uhn tawl laht/laiv …

Do you like sport?
An toil leat/leibh spòrs? inf/pol — uhn tawl laht/laiv sporsh

Do you like drama?
An toil leat/leibh uhn tawl laht/laiv
dràma? inf/pol *drah*·muh?

What kind of music do you like?
Dè an seòrsa ciùil as jen *shawr*·suh *kyoo*·il uhs
toil leat/leibh? inf/pol tawl laht/laiv

Do you have any children?
A' bheil clann agad/ uh vel klown *ah*·kuht/
agaibh? inf/pol *ah*·kif

Do you have a partner?
A' bheil cèile agad/ uh vel *keh*·luh *ah*·kuht/
agaibh? inf/pol *ah*·kif

I like ...
Is toil leam ... stawl luhm ...

I don't like ...
Cha toil leam ... hah tawl luhm ...

I'd like ...
Bu toil leam ... buh tawl luhm ...

I wouldn't like ...
Cha bu toil leam ... hah buh tawl luhm ...

Would you like ...?
Am bu toil leat/ uhm buh tawl laht/
leibh ... ? inf/pol laiv ...

Yes, I'd like that.
Bu toil. buh tawl

No, I wouldn't like that.
Cha bu toil. hah buh tawl

FESTIVAL TIME

The annual Gaelic arts festival, usually held in early October at different locations around Scotland, is known as *am Mòd* uhm mawt. It's a competition-based festival which celebrates the Gaelic language and culture through music, dance, drama, arts and literature. The Mòd attracts visitors and competitors from across the globe.

GOING OUT

What are you doing this evening?
   Dè tha thu/sibh a'   jeh hah oo/shif uh
   dèanamh feasgar? inf/pol   *jee*·uh·nuhv *fesk*·uhr

Would you like to go for a drink?
   Am bu toil leat/leibh   uhm buh tawl laht/laiv
   a dhol a ghabhail   uh ghawl uh *gah*·vuhl
   dràm? inf/pol   drahm

Would you like to go for a meal?
   Am bu toil leat/leibh a   uhm buh tawl laht/laiv uh
   dhol gu biadh? inf/pol   ghawl guh *bee*·uhgh

That'd be great.
   Bhiodh sin   *vee*·ugh shin
   sgoinneil.   *skawn*·yuhl

I'm sorry, I can't.
   Tha mi duilich, chan   hah mee *doo*·likh khahn
   urrainn dhomh.   *oo*·rin ghawm

WELL-WISHING

Happy birthday!
   Co-là breith   koh·lah breh
   sona dhut!   *soh*·nuh ghoot

Happy Christmas!
   Nollaig Chridheil!   *naw*·lik *khree*·uhl

Happy New Year!
   Bliadhna Mhath Ùr!   *blee*·uh·nuh vah oor

Congratulations!
   Meal do/ur naidheachd! inf/pol   myahl doh/oor *neh*·yahkhk

Good luck.
   Gun téid leat/leibh. inf/pol   goon chehj laht/laiv

FOOD & DRINK

Food

breakfast	*bracaist* f	*brah*·kishch
lunch	*lòn* m	lohn
dinner	*dìnnear* f	*jee*·nyuhr
drink	*deoch* f	jokh
food	*biadh* m	*bee*·uhgh
restaurant	*taigh-bidhe/*	tai·*bee*·uh/
	biadhlann m/f	*bee*·uh·luhn

What would you like?
   Dè tha thu ag iarraidh?   jeh hah oo uhk *ee*·uh·ree

Give me ..., please.
   Thoir dhomh ... mas   hawr ghawm ... mahsh
   e do thoil e.   eh duh hawl eh

I'd like ...
   Tha mi ag iarraidh ...   hah mee uhk *ee*·uh·ree ...

Are you hungry?
   A' bheil an t-acras ort?   uh vel uhn *tak*·ruhs awrsht

Are you thirsty?
   A' bheil am pathadh ort?   uh vel uhm *pah*·huhgh orsht

I'm hungry.
   Tha an t-acras orm.   hah uhn *tak*·ruhs *aw*·ruhm

I'm thirsty.
   Tha am pathadh orm.   hah uhn *pah*·huhgh *aw*·ruhm

I enjoyed that.
   Chòrd sin rium.   hawrsht shin ryoom

That was tasty.
   Bha sin blasta.   vah shin *blah*·stuh

That was really tasty.
   Bha sin deagh bhlasta.   vah shin joh *vlah*·stuh

I'd like some more.
   Tha mi ag iarraidh   hah mee uhk *ee*·uh·ree
   tuilleadh.   *too*·lyuhgh

beans	pònairean f pl	paw·nuh·ruhn
beef	feòil-mhairt f	fyawl·vahrsht
black pudding	marag dhubh f	mah·rahk ghoo
bread	aran m	ah·ruhn
chicken	cearc f	kyahrk
crab	crùbag f	kroo·puhk
dessert	mìlsean m	meel·shuhn
egg	ugh m	oo
eggs	uighean m pl	oo·yuhn
fish	iasg m	ee·uhsk
fruit	measan m pl	meh·suhn
herring	sgadan n	skah·duhn
lamb	feòil-uain f	fyawl oo·uhn
lobster	giomach m	gi·muhkh
meat	feòil f	fyawl
oatcakes	aran-coirce m	ah·ruhn·kawr·kyuh
peas	peasair f	pe·suhr
porridge (Lewis)	lite f	lee·chuh
porridge (Skye)	brochan m	braw·khuhn
potato	buntàta m	buhn·tah·tuh
salmon	bradan m	brah·tuhn
sandwich	pìos m	pees
soup	brot m	brawt
toast	tost f	tohst
vegetables	glasraich f	glahs·rikh
venison	sitheann f	shee·uhn

Drinks

milk	bainne m	bah·nyuh
orange juice	sùgh-orains m	soo·aw·rinsh
water	uisge m pl	oosh·kuh
(a cup of) coffee	(cupa) cofaidh …	(koo·puh) kaw·fee …
(a cup of) tea	(cupa) tì …	(koo·puh) tee …
with milk	le bainne	leh bah·nyuh
without milk	gun bhainne	goon vah·nyuh
with sugar	le siùcar	leh shoo·kuhr
without sugar	gun siùcar	goon shoo·kuhr

IN THE PUB

I'd like a …	Bu toil leam …	buh tawl luhm …
glass of red wine	glainne fìon dearg	glah·nyuh fee·uhn je·ruhk
glass of whisky	glainne uisge-beatha	glah·nyuh oosh·kuh·beh·huh
glass of white wine	glainne fìon geal	glah·nyuh fee·uhn gyahl
half-pint of beer	leth-phinnt leann	leh·feench lyown
pint of beer	pinnt leann	peench lyown

It's my round.
'Se an turas agamsa a tha ann.
sheh uhn *too*·ruhs *ah*·kuhm·suh hown

I'll get this one. (man speaking)
Gheobh mise am fear seo.
yoh *mee*·shuh uhm fehr shaw

I'll get this one. (woman speaking)
Gheobh mise an tè seo.
yoh *mee*·shuh uhn cheh shaw

What will you have?
Dè ghabhas tu/sibh? inf/pol
jeh *gah*·vuhs too/shif

The same again.
An aon rud a-rithist.
uhn ern root uh *ree*·ishch

I've had enough, thanks.
Tha gu leòr agam, tapadh leat/leibh. inf/pol
ha guh lyawr *ah*·kuhm tah·puh laht/laiv

Cheers!
Slàinte mhòr!
slahn·chuh vohr

PLACE NAMES

Aberdeen	*Obar Dheathain*	oh·puhr ehn
	(lit: mouth of-Don, ie the river Don)	
Edinburgh	*Dùn Éideann*	doon eh·juhn
	(lit: fort of-Éideann, or Edwin)	
Fort William	*An Gearasdan*	uhn gyeh·ruh·stuhn
	(lit: the garrison)	
Glasgow	*Glaschu*	glah·suh·khoo
Harris	*na Hearadh*	nuh he·ruhgh
the Highlands	*a' Ghàidhealtachd*	uh gheh·yuhl·tuhkhk
	(lit: the place-of-the-Gaels)	
Inverness	*Inbhir Nis*	in·vuhr nish
	(lit: outlet of-Ness)	
the Isle of Islay	*Ìle*	ee·luh
the Isle of Skye	*An t-Eilean*	uhn che·luhn
	Sgitheanach	skee·uh·nuhkh
	(lit: the winged island)	
Lewis	*Leòdhas*	lyoh·uhs
Oban	*An t-Òban*	uhn toh·buhn
	(lit: the small-bay)	
Portree	*Port Rìgh*	pawrsht ree
	(lit: harbour-of-the-king)	
Scotland	*Alba*	ah·luh·puh
Stornoway	*Steornabhaigh*	shchuhr·nuh·vai
Sutherland	*Cataibh*	kah·tif
Uist	*Uibhist*	oo·ishch

Cornish

Number of speakers: 3500

Key area: Cornwall, England

Notes: Cornish is a Celtic language related to Welsh and Breton. It ceased to function as a community language in the 18th century but was revived early in the 20th century.

Sounds: dh = 'th' in 'this' or 'that'
kh = 'ch' in 'loch'

1	*unn*	een
2	*dew/diw* m/f	dew/deew
3	*tri/teyr* m/f	tree/tair
4	*peswar/peder* m/f	*pez*·wahr/*pe*·der
5	*pymp*	pimp
6	*hwegh*	whaykh
7	*seyth*	saith
8	*eth*	ehth
9	*naw*	now
10	*deg*	daig

Good morning.
  Myttin da. — *mit*·teen da

Good day.
  Dydh da. — didh da

Good afternoon.
  Dohajydh da. — do·*ha*·jidh da

Good evening.
  Gorthugher da. — gawth·*ee*·her da

How are you?
  Fatla genes? — *fat*·la *gen*·nes

Very well, (thank you).
  Yn poynt da, (meur rasta). — in poynt da (mur *ras*·ta)

And you?
  Ha ty? — ha tee

Good night!
  Nos dha! — nawz dha

Goodbye. (to one person)
  Dyw genes. — dew *gen*·nes

Goodbye. (to more than one person)
  Dyw genowgh. — dew *gen*·nohkh

Can you speak Cornish?
  A wodhesta kewsel — a *wo*·dhes·ta *kew*·zel
  Kernewek? — kur·*new*·ek

Yes, I speak a little.
  Gonn, y kewsav boghes. — gon a *kew*·zaf *bow*·khez

Cornish

233

No, I can't speak Cornish very well.
Na wonn, ny gowsav   nah won nee *go*·zaf
Kernewek yn ta.   kur·*new*·ek in ta

Do you understand?
A wodhesta konvedhes?   a *wo*·dhes·ta kon·*ve*·dhez

Yes, I understand.
Gonn, my a gonvedh.   gon mee a *gon*·vedh

No, I don't understand.
Na wonn, ny gonvedhav.   nah won nee gon·*ve*·dhaf

Scots (Lallans)

Note that because Lallans is spelt the way it's pronounced, there are no separate pronunciation guides in this section.

1	*ae/ane*	6	*sax*
2	*twa*	7	*sieven*
3	*three*	8	*aicht*
4	*fower*	9	*nine*
5	*five*	10	*ten*

Good morning.	*Guid mornin.*
Good day.	*Guid day.*
Good afternoon.	*Guid efter nune.*
Good evening.	*Guid e'en.*
Good night.	*Guid nicht.*
Goodbye.	*Fare ye weel.*
How are you?	*Hou's aw wi ye?*
Fine, thank you.	*Guid, thank ye.*
I can't complain.	*A canna compleen.*
And you?	*And yersel?*
Come back soon.	*Haste ye back.*
Can you speak Lallans?	*Can ye speak Lallans?*
Yes, I speak a little.	*Aye, a wee bit.*
No, I can't speak Lallans very well.	*No, ah canna speak Lallans very weel.*
Do you understand?	*Dae ye unnerstaun?*
Yes, I understand.	*Aye, ah unnerstaun.*
No, I don't understand.	*No, ah dinnae unnerstaun.*

WORDFINDER

E

F

N

T

What kind of traveller are you?

A. You're eating chicken for dinner *again* because it's the only word you know.

B. When no one understands what you say, you step closer and shout louder.

C. When the barman doesn't understand your order, you point frantically at the beer.

D. You're surrounded by locals, swapping jokes, email addresses and experiences – other travellers want to borrow your phrasebook or audio guide.

If you answered A, B, or C, you NEED Lonely Planet's language products ...

- **Lonely Planet Phrasebooks** – for every phrase you need in every language you want

- **Lonely Planet Language & Culture** – get behind the scenes of English as it's spoken around the world – learn and laugh

- **Lonely Planet Fast Talk & Fast Talk Audio** – essential phrases for short trips and weekends away – read, listen and talk like a local

- **Lonely Planet Small Talk** – 10 essential languages for city breaks

- **Lonely Planet Real Talk** – downloadable language audio guides from lonelyplanet.com to your MP3 player

... and this is why

- **Talk to everyone everywhere**
  Over 120 languages, more than any other publisher

- **The right words at the right time**
  Quick-reference colour sections, two-way dictionary, easy pronunciation, every possible subject – and audio to support it

Lonely Planet Offices

Australia
90 Maribyrnong St, Footscray,
Victoria 3011
☎ 03 8379 8000
fax 03 8379 8111
✉ talk2us@lonelyplanet.com.au

USA
150 Linden St, Oakland,
CA 94607
☎ 510 893 8555
fax 510 893 8572
✉ info@lonelyplanet.com

UK
72-82 Rosebery Ave,
London EC1R 4RW
☎ 020 7841 9000
fax 020 7841 9001
✉ go@lonelyplanet.co.uk

lonelyplanet.com